Praise for

To Love and Be Loved

"Jim Towey's *To Love and Be Loved: A Personal Portrait of Mother Teresa* is the loveliest book I've read in recent months, rich in reflection on contemporary sanctity and including one of the Five Funniest Catholic Stories Ever."

—George Weigel

"Towey recounts the hours Mother Teresa spent daily in deep prayer as well as the cheerfulness and compassion with which she served people in crushing poverty. . . . [His] retelling of his beloved friend's persistent dark night of the soul makes the reader want to comfort her. . . . Readers familiar with Mother Teresa's biography will find fresh meaning in Towey's account of her impact on his spiritual journey. Those unfamiliar with her life story will appreciate his accessible and gripping introduction."

—*America* magazine

"*To Love and Be Loved: A Personal Portrait of Mother Teresa* is a powerful 'white pill,' masterfully weaving together vignettes from Towey's own life with the arc of the Albanian nun pursuing the will of God."

—*The Washington Free Beacon*

"Towey portrays Mother Teresa in trademark sandals and sari, and also as a human who experienced loneliness, wrestled with doubts, and loved sweets. . . . This personal portrait is by turns autobiographical, biographical, and devotional. Especially moving are the stories of Mother Teresa's vivid calling through a vision, her dark night of the soul, and her final decline."

—Booklist

"Though Towey's personal, transformative relationship with Mother Teresa forms the central theme, he also offers a fascinating inside look into Mother Teresa's daily life. . . . Inspiring and joyful."

—Kirkus Reviews

TO LOVE
AND
BE LOVED

A Personal Portrait of
MOTHER TERESA

JIM TOWEY

Simon & Schuster Paperbacks

New York London Toronto Sydney New Delhi

Simon & Schuster Paperbacks
An Imprint of Simon & Schuster, Inc.
1230 Avenue of the Americas
New York, NY 10020

Photo Credits: Trinity Mirror/Mirrorpix/Alamy Stock Photo; Mary Ellen Mark/
The Mary Ellen Mark Foundation; Tim Graham/Hulton Archive via Getty Images;
Francois Lochon/Gamma-Rapho via Getty Images; Ira Wyman/Sygma via Getty
Images; Tim Graham/Tim Graham Photo Library via Getty Images; Courtesy of
Prasad Photography Newport Beach; Courtesy of Prasad Photography Newport
Beach; Courtesy of Michael Collopy; New York Daily News Archive/New York Daily
News via Getty Images; Marc Deville/Gamma-Rapho via Getty Images; Hiroki
Ogawa (Creative Commons License); Courtesy of Michael Collopy

First Simon & Schuster trade paperback edition September 2023

SIMON & SCHUSTER PAPERBACKS and colophon are registered
trademarks of Simon & Schuster, Inc.

For information about special discounts for bulk purchases,
please contact Simon & Schuster Special Sales at 1-866-506-1949
or business@simonandschuster.com.

The Simon & Schuster Speakers Bureau can bring authors to
your live event. For more information or to book an event,
contact the Simon & Schuster Speakers Bureau at 1-866-248-3049
or visit our website at www.simonspeakers.com.

Interior design by Lewelin Polanco

Manufactured in the United States of America

10 9 8 7 6 5 4 3 2 1

Library of Congress Cataloging-in-Publication Data
has been applied for.

ISBN 978-1-9821-9562-5
ISBN 978-1-9821-9563-2 (pbk)
ISBN 978-1-9821-9564-9 (ebook)

In honor of Mary, the Mother of God

Then the King will say to those on his right hand, "Come, you whom my Father has blessed, take for your heritage the kingdom prepared for you since the foundation of the world. For I was hungry and you gave me food; I was thirsty and you gave me drink; I was a stranger and you made me welcome; naked and you clothed me, sick and you visited me, in prison and you came to see me." Then the virtuous will say to him in reply, "Lord, when did we see you hungry and feed you; or thirsty and give you drink? When did we see you a stranger and make you welcome; naked and clothe you; sick or in prison and go to see you?" And the King will answer, "I tell you solemnly, in so far as you did this to one of the least of these brothers of mine, you did it to me."

—Matthew 25:34–40

Contents

TO LOVE
AND
BE LOVED

The Mother I Knew

A life not lived for others is not worth living.

—*Mother Teresa*

September 13, 1997

It was 2 a.m. when I arrived at Saint Thomas Church in Calcutta on the day of Mother Teresa's state funeral. I had landed hours earlier with the other members of the official U.S. delegation led by First Lady Hillary Clinton. My fellow delegates had gone off to catch up on sleep, though two sisters of the Missionaries of Charity who had flown with us went straight to the motherhouse to join the hundreds of their fellow MCs converging upon the city.

Queens, presidents, dignitaries, and celebrities from all over the world had come to attend the funeral, including the anchors of the three American television networks and CNN. (The same international press corps had covered Princess Diana's funeral a week earlier.) Every high-end hotel in the city was filled to capacity. The U.S. delegation was split between the two finest—the Oberoi and the Taj Bengal—but I had no interest in sleep. I wanted to get as near as possible to Mother.

Even at that early hour, there was a crowd milling about outside the 150-year-old church, and dozens of sisters were in quiet conversation near the entrance. Mother had lain in state here, draped in an Indian flag, for a week, and hundreds of thousands of well-wishers had filed past her body. She would ride to her final resting place on the same gun carriage that carried Mohandas Gandhi's body in 1948. There were military personnel and city police at the ready, though the sisters were doing a fine job guarding Mother themselves. I entered the sanctuary of the church and saw a good number of them keeping vigil, and I joined them. There were few dry eyes in the sanctuary.

Mother Teresa looked remarkably well preserved. The team of embalmers from Bombay who had come to Calcutta immediately after her death could be proud. Their efforts were aided by six hastily installed air conditioners that fought bravely to counteract the punishing subtropical heat. Still, her face was somewhat ashen, and her hands and feet a little discolored. Her darker complexion made her look Indian. She was dressed in her trademark sari, and her rosary— which in times past she would swap with mine when we prayed on a car trip—stretched from her hands, resting on her stomach. Her body seemed sacred. On the night Mother died, Sister Gertrude had carefully withdrawn vials of blood from Mother to preserve it for reliquary. (I was later given a blood relic.) A sister had given me several medals when I first came to the foot of Mother's coffin. I took these medals, and my rosary, and touched them to her bare feet. Now, as I knelt before her body, I could grieve freely, and I did. These were not all tears of sadness. I was overcome with gratitude to God and to this woman who had given me so much joy.

Just as the Roman calendar is separated into eras before and after the birth of Christ, so my life can be fairly divided into two distinct periods: before and after Mother. Meeting her not only reshaped how I thought and acted, but ultimately determined every significant choice I made, from the jobs I have taken, to the woman I married, to the house we live in, to how I spend my days. I knew Mother during the last twelve years of her life, from 1985 until her death in 1997. I was her lawyer, and legal counsel for the Missionaries of Charity (work I continue to do), but more important, I was her friend, and Mother was mine. She guided me on matters big and small and allowed me to help her where I could. She showed me that everyday moments offer the greatest opportunity to serve God by doing "small things with great love." It is no exaggeration to say that she taught me how to live and love.

So many memories rushed to mind as I knelt at Mother's feet in Saint Thomas Church. All the joys I had known with my wife and our children could be traced back to that fateful day in 1985 when Mother welcomed me in Calcutta and sent me to Kalighat, her Home for the Dying. She brought me to Jesus—not the concept of Jesus, not the historical figure of twenty centuries ago, but the living God whom I could access by faith.

I thought, too, of all the friends I had made because of her. Many of the people I cherished most I had only met because they were close to Mother: Sandy McMurtrie, for instance, and the filmmaker Jan Petrie. Naresh and Sunita Kumar, the Calcutta couple who were like family to Mother, had become family to me. I thought of the many MC sisters I had come to know and love over the years, as well as the MC fathers with whom I had lived in Tijuana and who were my brothers for life.

Most of all, though, I thought of the "poorest of the poor," from the many dying men and women I came to know at the Gift of Peace AIDS home to the soup-kitchen regulars across town whom I befriended. Mother referred to the neediest as "Jesus in His distressing disguise of the poorest of the poor." She based this belief on the actual presence of God in the person of the poor on the teaching of Jesus recorded in Matthew's Gospel:

> For I was hungry and you gave me food; I was thirsty and you gave me drink . . . sick and you visited me. . . . In so far as you did this to one of the least of these brothers of mine, you did it to me.

This passage was central to the mission of the Missionaries of Charity, and Mother made a point of working the words "you did it to me" into nearly every public or private talk I heard her give. Her faith told her she interacted with God whenever she helped the poor, which was why she distinguished the work she and her sisters did from social work. She once said in an interview, "The work is only the expression of the love we have for God. We have to pour our love on someone. And the people are the means of expressing our love."

My relationships with the people the Missionaries of Charity served had Mother Teresa's fingerprints on them. There was no chance I would ever have met them without Mother's invitation to touch "Jesus in His distressing disguise," which, by degree, I slowly came to realize they were.

Memories of them constitute some of the most graphic proofs to me of the loving presence of God in the world, of the ocean of mercy that engulfs the willing and unwilling alike, and of the debt I owe Mother Teresa for changing the entire trajectory of my life. This realization descended upon me in waves of gratitude in Saint Thomas Church, but also sadness. She was gone for good, no longer a phone call or plane ride away.

As I prayed in the early hours of September 13, 1997, I was hounded by a simple question that had nagged me for some time: Why me? Why did I get to have this privileged relationship with Mother Teresa? I surely didn't deserve it. I know the sinner I was on the day I met her, and how I felt at Kalighat, helping a sick man not through any good purpose, but because I was too proud to admit to the sister in charge that I didn't want to touch him. I am still that same sinner. So why me? I didn't have an answer that night, but I do now.

I believe God gave me Mother Teresa for three reasons. First, because I needed her desperately. I was a sinner, who loved earthly pleasure and who might have spent these last thirty-seven years indulging myself had it not been for Mother and the graces from above that she revealed. My life was purposeless, and she took me in. Her love and kindness during those first years helped me acknowledge my own brokenness and need for God, and His healing touch. In a way, she nursed me back to life. She taught me to pray, love the word of God, and frequent the Church's sacraments because she knew that if I didn't, I would grow lost again.

And she gave me the MCs, the poor entrusted to them, and the wonderful people drawn to volunteer in their service, so I would be in good company and not stray. Mother's love revealed to me my vocation. Her maternal heart helped me embrace it. And this is the second reason God brought me to Mother, so I could help the MCs after she was gone. I have kept the pledge I made when I visited her in the hospital and will keep it until my services are no longer needed or valuable.

Finally, I am convinced that my experiences with Mother, and my observations of the last twelve years of her life, were meant to benefit others. The lessons I learned from her about living, loving, and aging, and how to come closer to God, deserve to be shared.

People need to know the Mother I knew.

This book is the story of the Mother Teresa I observed, studied, and followed. Many others were closer to her, especially the members of her Missionaries of Charity family. And I am particularly conscious of the fact that chronicling my relationship with Mother might appear to exploit our friendship (for the record, I will not financially benefit from this book—the royalties will be donated to her sisters, priests, and other charities aligned with her life's work). My purpose in writing this book is to show her as I knew her—not as the perfect, plastic saint that she inevitably became in the minds of some people, but the real person who had friends and liked chocolate and told jokes and occasionally got angry. Seeing her humanity, with all the sweetness and frailty that entails, makes her life and works all the more remarkable.

I have kept personal journals throughout my life, and I took copious and contemporaneous notes during my years with Mother. I wanted to remember and be able to tell my children. I also have boxes of correspondence and other material arising from my legal representation of her (the Mother Teresa Center, the organization the Missionaries of Charity tasked with promoting and protecting her legacy, granted me permission to share this information). The stories here are based on those journals and files, as well as hours of interviews I conducted with her friends and sisters, especially those who were with her at the founding of the Missionaries of Charity.

Mother has been gone for twenty-five years now, and this book is intended to bear witness to the person she was. I hope you will get a sense of what it meant to be friends with a living saint: how humbling and challenging—and at times frustrating—it was to be in the presence of someone so in love with God. She was a holy woman and the tenderest of mothers, and it was the great blessing of my life to know her and serve with her.

CHAPTER 1

Calcutta

The poor are the hope and salvation of mankind.

—*Mother Teresa*

The easiest way to understand Mother Teresa is through Calcutta. The twentieth century was one of great political upheaval for the vast Indian metropolis, compounded by floods, famine, and numerous refugee crises. During her first decade in the city, the population nearly doubled; by the time she died in 1997, it had nearly doubled again. Calcutta has come a long way in the last twenty-five years, but millions still live in poverty, without adequate food or medical care, in sanitary conditions unimaginable to most Americans.

But where others saw squalor and misery and privation, Mother Teresa saw the children of God, created in His image. She saw dignity, something precious, in everyone. In even Calcutta's poorest, she recognized the longing to be wanted. The city's desperate need made Mother Teresa who she was. Its abandoned children and lepers reached out for help, and she was mother to them all. Calcutta, with all its suffering, was her spiritual home, the place where she created something beautiful for God.

I was twenty-eight, a lawyer and a senior advisor to Oregon senator Mark Hatfield, when I met Mother Teresa. My boss was chairman of the Senate Appropriations Committee, and such an influential position brings perks for the staff. During the 1985 summer recess, I was sent on a fact-finding mission to Malaysia, Hong Kong, and the Thai-Cambodian border. Hatfield had been the only senator to vote against U.S. military involvement in Vietnam, and after the war ended, he was the leader in Congress on refugee protection and resettlement. He felt our country had a moral obligation to those who faced persecution for helping the U.S. military. I was sent to see the Indochinese refugee camps where we were processing thousands of claims for resettlement and expending hundreds of millions of dollars.

Hatfield was a devout Southern Baptist and had been friends with Mother Teresa since the early 1970s, long before she became a household name. She had visited his office on Capitol Hill just before I joined. Since my official business had me in her neighborhood, a swing through Calcutta for a courtesy meeting was easy to arrange, and my boss gave me the introduction I needed.

Like everyone, I knew her as a holy woman who lived among the poor, helping desperate people few bothered to notice. Pope John Paul II, whom I admired greatly, had taken a special interest in her work and was often photographed with her. And I had friends in Washington, Jan and Randy Sterns, who had adopted a child from one of Mother Teresa's orphanages in India. Natasha Gabriella was an energetic, cheerful little girl, and seeing her brought thoughts of Mother Teresa's work to the fore. On Jan's recommendation, I read Malcolm Muggeridge's book about her, *Something Beautiful for God*. Muggeridge had a somewhat cynical take on organized religion—a take I identified with—so his admiration of Mother made me even more curious. The response of this agnostic to his sojourn with her was striking: "For those of us who find difficulty in grasping with our minds Christ's great propositions of love . . . someone like Mother Teresa is a godsend. She is this love in person; through her, we can reach it, and hold it, and incorporate it in ourselves." She and her work in India had clearly touched him deeply.

I looked forward to telling people that I had been to Calcutta and met Mother Teresa. That was the ostensible reason for my side trip. But, secretly, I hoped she could somehow heal me, as Jesus healed the blind men. Despite my great job and wide circle of friends, my life in Washington felt hollow. It was the opposite of everything Muggeridge had written about the life of his newfound friend: She was joyfully, enthusiastically living the Christian Gospel and the Catholic faith. I hoped that meeting her in person might reignite my spiritual life and set me back on course, just as it seemed to have done for Muggeridge.

I had always called myself a Catholic. Religion was the life preserver that kept me afloat through a turbulent childhood. My parents had separated when I was in fourth grade. My mother raised five children in Jacksonville, Florida, and she made sure we went to Catholic schools and got to church on Sundays. Her sincere faith and lovely piety made a strong impression on me. But by the time I got to Florida State

University in 1974, my being Catholic and going to church every week was more about making myself interesting to girls than it was about having a true relationship with God. The parts of Church teaching that made demands on me, I simply ignored. I was foul-mouthed if it got me a laugh; enjoyed gambling, drinking, and sexual pleasure; and thought nothing of lying to others to get around a problem.

Any sense of sin was dulled by my familiarity with it. Pascal described it best: "Sinners lick the earth, that is to say, love earthly pleasures." I had licked the earth. In my selfish pursuits, I had hurt people who genuinely loved me, including my college girlfriend, whose heart broke when I didn't marry her. I was a comfortable, cultural Catholic who held God under my command.

But nine months before my trip to Southeast Asia, God woke me up. My friend Jimmy committed suicide. He was a real competitor: a six-foot-six small forward on the FSU basketball team, but also a 4.0 student in philosophy. He was a lover of classic literature and a practicing Catholic, and we connected on every level. We were inseparable. We went to discos and pubs, played golf and tennis, sunned ourselves at the beach and double-dated. We were members of the same fraternity, took our summer vacations together, and tried to outdo each other in offbeat humor. I was the best man when he married his beautiful college sweetheart. Not even five years later, in a fit of despair, he jumped off an Interstate 95 overpass in Lantana, Florida, into southbound traffic.

I had failed my friend. I knew Jimmy was struggling; he was drinking too much, and his last visit to D.C. had been a disaster. Everything was dark and discouraging to him, from his recent divorce to his failed attempts to land a job as head coach for a basketball team. He was on a roller coaster that wouldn't let him off. One minute he was on his knees crying and asking God for help, and the next he was back to obsessing about his ex-wife and foundering career. He arrived at my apartment a mess and left a few days later in worse shape. But instead of going straight to Florida when Jimmy called me almost desperate, ranting incoherently, just a week before his suicide, I had stayed in Washington. And now he was gone. I was haunted by guilt, and my faith was shaken. How could a loving God let all this happen? Where was He when Jimmy was suffering? Why didn't He send me to the rescue?

In the months after Jimmy's death, I threw myself into my work. I prayed less, and I drank more. I cultivated a snide cynicism, nurtured by the phony social rituals and mercenary friendships of Capitol Hill. My hypocrisy allowed me to spot it instantly in others. Outwardly, I might have seemed a great guy—successful at work, fun to be around, and, by all appearances, religious. I even dabbled in tutoring inner-city kids once a week, which soothed my conscience and impressed other people. I was my little brother's keeper for two whole hours a week. I had everyone fooled. But I couldn't fool myself.

This was the man who sought Mother Teresa in August 1985. She was living the Gospel and practicing the faith that I had been taught as a child. I hoped if I met her, she could ease my guilt over Jimmy and point me toward a more meaningful life. I thought she might tell me to become a priest. Most of my friends were marrying, and since I had no desire to commit myself to a woman for life, I wondered if

God wanted me in the seminary. Such thoughts show how truly lost I was. I was grasping for answers and increasingly convinced that if I could just be with Mother Teresa for a moment, she might provide them to me.

I needed to go to Calcutta.

Agnes Gonxha Bojaxhiu was born August 26, 1910, in Skopje, North Macedonia, then part of the Ottoman Empire. The tiny girl known by her middle name, Gonxha (meaning "flower bud"), was drawn to stories of missionaries from an early age and was only eighteen when she informed her mother that she felt called by God. She wanted to be a missionary in India "to go out and give the life of Christ to the people." It would require courage and great sacrifice, but she had a toughness born of tragedy.

Gonxha had grown up ethnic Albanian and Catholic in a predominantly Muslim and Orthodox Christian community in modern-day North Macedonia. Her mother, Drana, was a deeply religious and highly self-disciplined woman who had a well-earned reputation for caring for the poor. She never turned away the needy and often gave them a meal, explaining to her children that the poor were also part of their family. Gonxha's father happily bankrolled his wife's generosity. Nikola was a successful merchant whose building and trade activities took him as far as Egypt. He was also a passionate Albanian nationalist, active in the movement demanding independence from Turkish rule. This hobby was not without risk; politics in the Ottoman Empire at the end of World War I were volatile. In 1919, he traveled to a dinner meeting of political activists in Belgrade, where he was poisoned. When he returned home gravely ill, eight-year-old Gonxha was sent to find a priest to administer the last rites to her dying father. The priest arrived in the Bojaxhiu home in time to anoint Nikola before he was rushed to the hospital, where he died.

Immediately following Nikola's death, the Bojaxhiu family found themselves with nothing more than the roof over their heads, as all of Nikola's business assets were appropriated by his Italian business partner. It was only Drana's fortitude and enterprise that pulled the family through. She sold handcrafted embroidery and other cloth materials to provide for the family's needs, as well as the needs of the poor who continued to come to their door.

After so much loss, Gonxha knew her choice to leave home would be a heavy cross for her mother to bear. But her mother gave her blessing, telling her daughter, "Put your hand in Jesus' hand, and walk alone with Him. Walk ahead, because if you look back you will go back." Her daughter would never forget her courage or her advice.

Gonxha wept as the train pulled away from Skopje on September 26, 1928. Her mother accompanied her as far as Zagreb, where they said their final goodbyes. They would never see each other again. Many years later, Mother Teresa said that when it was time for her to die and be judged, she would be measured by how well she'd honored the sacrifice she demanded of her own mother: "My mother will judge me. She did not accept my going. I think of her when I'm tempted. What would she say?"

After a brief stop in Paris for an interview with a Loreto

nun to whom she had been recommended by a Skopje priest, Gonxha arrived at the headquarters of the Sisters of Loreto in Dublin. The Institute of the Blessed Virgin Mary, commonly known as the Sisters of Loreto, is a religious order focused on teaching and evangelism. Gonxha stayed in Ireland studying English for about six weeks, and on December 1, 1928, she began a five-week voyage to India, where the Sisters had a long-established presence.

As she sailed away from her life in Europe, she composed a poem she called "Farewell." She described herself as "Christ's happy little one" traveling toward "steamy Bengal" and "torrid India." The final stanza gives a glimpse of the price she paid to leave all she loved for an unknown land:

> Fine and pure as summer dew
> Her soft warm tears begin to flow,
> Sealing and sanctifying now
> Her painful sacrifice.

She spent Christmas without a Mass because there was no priest on board the ship, but one boarded at a stop in Sri Lanka, which made for a prayerful New Year's celebration. She set foot on Indian soil in Madras. Nothing in her childhood had prepared her for the shock of what she saw. She recorded her first impressions for the diocesan magazine back home:

> Many families live in the streets, along the city walls, even in places thronged with people. Day and night they live out in the open on mats they have made

from large palm leaves—or frequently on the bare ground. They are all virtually naked, wearing at best a ragged loincloth. . . . As we went along the street we chanced upon one family gathered around a dead relation, wrapped in worn red rags, strewn with yellow flowers, his face painted in colored stripes. It was a horrifying scene. If our people could only see all of this, they would stop grumbling about their own misfortunes and offer thanks to God for blessing them with such abundance.

She reached Calcutta on January 6, 1929, the feast of the Epiphany—the day Christians celebrate the universality of Christ's birth and message. This coincidence was fitting for the girl who would become the most celebrated missionary of the age.

She spent her initial years in India at a convent at Darjeeling, high in the foothills of the Himalayas, studying Scripture, theology, and Catholic teachings. She took her first vows in May 1931 and became Sister Teresa, choosing to name herself after Thérèse of Lisieux. Nicknamed the "Little Flower," Saint Thérèse had, as Mother Teresa later described it, a way of "doing small things with great love" and provided the model for her life.

After vows, Sister Teresa was sent to the Loreto community in Calcutta's Entally neighborhood, to teach at Saint Mary's School. In a letter she sent home, she described her "indescribable happiness" at being in Calcutta. She shared with her friends back in Skopje her impressions of her new home and the price she was paying in her quest to save souls.

The heat of India is simply burning. When I walk around, it seems to me that fire is under my feet from which even my whole body is burning. When it is hardest, I console myself with the thought that souls are saved in this way and that dear Jesus has suffered much more for them. . . . The life of a missionary is not strewn with roses, in fact more with thorns; but with it all, it is a life full of happiness and joy when she thinks that she is doing the same work which Jesus was doing when He was on earth, and that she is fulfilling Jesus' commandment: "Go and teach all nations."

She barely left Calcutta for the next thirty years, only occasionally having to travel in the wider Bengal region. She spent the vast majority of her life in that city, teaching and ministering to its poorest.

Calcutta was not always the scene of misery and chaos its name brings to mind. Founded in 1686, it was the proud capital of British India and a thriving hub of trade for two centuries. The British built a Western-style city with commercial and government buildings, large homes, parks, long avenues, streetcars, and public utilities. But in 1911, they moved their capitol to New Delhi, and Calcutta saw its power and influence begin to decline. By the time Mother Teresa arrived in 1929, Calcutta was showing signs of decay. The process would be accelerated in the years to come by religious strife, war, and communal violence—and by an ever-burgeoning population. A succession of floods, famines, and refugee migrations would slowly overwhelm the city's infrastructure.

Despite such woes, Calcutta remained a vibrant cultural center throughout the upheavals of the twentieth century, and it continues to be the intellectual center of the nation. Authors, poets, philosophers, and masters of faith have made Calcutta a home for the aesthetically inclined. This combination of beauty and brokenness inspired Mother Teresa, and she made the city her canvas. She allowed its needs to feed her compassion and the fire of her Christian faith. Without the captivating contrasts of the city in which she labored—the vibrancy of its culture and the intensity of its suffering—she might never have captured the world's imagination. It was as though the abandoned children and lepers of the city made her a mother, and their need created her heroic capacity to serve. But there were limits to what even she could do. Her good intentions were always overwhelmed by the magnitude of the need that suffocated the city. A need that could never be met.

I feared that in my quest to see Mother Teresa, I, too, would be overwhelmed. Mother and her sisters had labored for thirty-five years to reach the destitute, but her patchwork of programs did not stretch nearly far enough. She described their work as a "drop in the ocean." There is simply no way to go to Calcutta and escape exposure to the pavement dwellers, beggars, and miserably poor. I was fearful of sinking into the quicksand of the city's abject poverty and had planned a five-day stopover in Hawaii on my way home from India as a reward for my courage.

My plane from Bangkok landed in Calcutta at Dum

Dum Airport as the sun was rising. I retrieved my bags and, still at the airport, was engulfed by everything I feared: barefoot children pleading for money, mothers dressed in rags with babies and outstretched hands, wiry men grabbing for my luggage, cows roaming the terminal, and, worst of all, no sign of my ride from the U.S. consulate.

I had no rupees, no Bengali, and no friends—just regret that I had come at all.

As I looked for my ride, street kids surrounded me, gesturing toward their mouths to say they were hungry. They called me "Uncle, Uncle" and repeated the only other English word they seemed to know, "money," sometimes tugging at the pockets of my pants. Eye contact only made them more frantic, so I tried my best to look through them as I batted grubby hands away and kept moving.

When it was clear to me a consular official was not going to ride up and whisk me away, I marched, bags firmly in hand, over to the area where cabs were lined up. With a phony display of confidence, I picked a driver at random and loaded my bags into the back of his ancient Ambassador-model cab.

I had picked a lemon. Minutes after we left, the car broke down. It rolled to a stop on a dirt road somewhere along the fifteen-mile route from the airport to the city. The driver angrily spoke words that had the unmistakable, international sound of cursing, and I harmonized in English. I soon found myself with both hands on the back of the vehicle, pushing to see if some movement would get it to start. I realized that if I succeeded, the cabbie might drive off with my luggage, which, at that point, seemed a fitting addition to the morning.

But the car coughed back to life, I jumped in, and we headed south to the city. From the exhaust cloud in the back seat, I shouted "New Kenilworth Hotel, Little Russell Road," over and over, hoping the volume and repetition would surmount the language barrier. In every direction, I saw bodies, young and old, lying on the pavement and dirt. Even at this early hour, it was already sweltering and bustling. People shouted, police whistles screamed, birds scavenged among the refuse scattered everywhere. There was an incessant blaring of horns from cabs as they jostled with rickshaw drivers, bicyclists, and barefoot men pulling wagons. Add in the smell of raw sewage and burning garbage, and you can imagine this hellish tableau. This panorama of agony was overwhelming for a white-bread congressional staffer. I felt I could have fallen off the face of the earth at any moment, never to be found. The cabbie located the hotel, but my $20 bill was useless to him. The hotel clerk inside allowed me to exchange some U.S. currency so I could pay properly, and with that, my odyssey from the airport to the hotel was complete.

The New Kenilworth Hotel was old, and my room had only a fan to stir the humidity and heat. As I wasn't scheduled to go to the Missionaries of Charity's headquarters until the next morning, I needed something to do with myself. I decided on a walk around the neighborhood before the afternoon rains started. I knew this would subject me to more beggary and filth, but having discovered at the airport my capacity to ignore human suffering, I thought I could handle it. I wanted to experience the feel of the streets, as I had done in Brussels and Bangkok.

But this adventure was as ill-fated as my arrival. There were no street markers or traffic signals, almost none of the building signage was in English, and I couldn't understand a word anyone was saying. I was lost within minutes.

Trying to retrace my steps simply made matters worse. I wandered for hours, sweat soaking through my clothes. The indistinguishable shops, ramshackle houses, crowded hovels, and hammer-and-sickle signs of the local Communist government created a maze of identical corners and alleys. Laughing children ran and played, oblivious to their squalid surroundings. Men wrapped in the traditional Indian dhoti bathed at a pump of running water. Others brushed their teeth along the curb or cooked food over charcoal fires mere feet from where garbage sat rotting.

What struck me was how busy everyone seemed to be. There wasn't the idleness you may see in the slums of the United States. There were other things you don't see in America: dogs pitiably emaciated and covered with mange and lesions; goats tethered to a rope under the watchful gaze of a shop owner whose store was also his home; Muslim women in black burkas; Hindu women in saris with red dots on their foreheads and bare stomachs; men lying along curbs, faces to the pavement, sleeping, sick, possibly dead; and cows stopping traffic as they searched for pastures nowhere to be found. The overcrowding everywhere, the sheer density of Calcutta's population, was like nothing I had ever seen anywhere. It felt like a baptism of fire.

Eventually, a well-dressed businessman who spoke English gave me directions to my hotel. As I drew near its entrance, another English-speaking Indian approached me.

He asked if I wanted female company. He pointed to a girl standing a short distance away who could not have been fifteen years old. I glared at him and walked quickly to my hotel's entrance, sickened. I had had enough of Calcutta for one day. I regretted not booking a room at the only nice hotel, the Oberoi, which was nearby in the market district. But after the misery I had seen on the streets, my room with its cockroaches and ceiling fan felt palatial.

In bed that night, I tried to cope with what I had seen, heard, and smelled. It was the rickshaw pullers that I couldn't get off my mind. They all looked the same: short, thin, and muscular in the most wiry way. Their skin was baked dark brown, their faces were filthy, their teeth rotting. Barefoot, they were always in a hurry and wove their way through stalled traffic, pulling passengers in the carriage behind them. Some observers referred to them as "human horses" because of how they bore their burdens at a slow trot.

Frommer's India on $25 a Day was the popular travel guide at the time. It attempted to acknowledge the moral and ethical dimension to the rickshaw puller's plight:

A rickshaw—if your conscience can stand this example of imperialist exploitation—is marvelous for an even closer viewing [of street life]. And however you feel about rickshaws, they're an intimate way to see the action. (To socially conscious Westerners who complain about how rickshaws "exploit human dignity," one local editor replied succinctly, "Well, if everybody refuses to hire them the problem will solve itself: they'll all starve to death.")

Calcutta is not an easy place. For me, it has always been full of moral and spiritual challenges. On that first trip, the city forced me to walk through streets full of suffering and filth. It paraded everything I was dreading. Much of what I saw scared me, and a lot of it disgusted me. But after a day in the midst of the rickshaw pullers and the hungry children and the men bathing in the street, I was no longer so afraid.

In revealing itself to me, Calcutta was helping me see myself better, too. It was stripping me of my pride. I had more in common with the beggars than I wanted to acknowledge. The difference was that their imperfections were on full display while mine were hidden. Despite my newfound gratitude for my filthy hotel room, it couldn't provide the respite I wished for; I was acutely aware that the man in the mirror was not as worldly-wise as I had thought. I was forced to encounter all that was disordered, filthy, and broken in me.

CHAPTER 2

Meeting Mother

Accept whatever He gives, and give whatever He takes, with a big smile.

—*Mother Teresa*

My second morning in Calcutta began at 5 a.m, but I had been awake for hours. I had tossed and turned all night in my hot, damp hotel room, overwhelmed by the city and nervous about my appointment. I was going to meet Mother Teresa, my whole reason for coming to Calcutta.

I was already sweating when I got down to the lobby, where a driver from the consulate was waiting to take me to the 6 a.m. Mass at the motherhouse of the Missionaries of Charity, the convent headquarters of the religious congregation. My meeting was scheduled for immediately after the service. The clean, orderly compound was a relief after the filth and chaos of the city. The chapel was on the second floor, and it was packed with hundreds of nuns in identical blue-striped white saris. I scanned the crowd for Mother Teresa, but it was impossible to tell which tiny covered head was hers. I found a spot with the volunteers and tourists in the far-right corner of the chapel and sat along the back wall, craning my neck to catch a glimpse of the service.

The chapel's windows overlooking Lower Circular Road were open, but offered little relief from the heat and humidity. They did let in waves of exhaust fumes, though, and the screeches of the trams and the cries of the blackbirds on the building's ledges. But this cacophony could not detract from the loveliness of the sisters singing their praises to God as Mass began. Here were true "choirs of angels."

The scriptural readings at Catholic Masses are not chosen locally. They are taken from the Lectionary, an extensive collection of Bible passages selected long ago by the Vatican. The selections are followed in order, without exception, year after year, all over the world. Weekday Masses include a reading from one of the four Gospels, preceded by an Old or New Testament selection. This Mass was on the "Tuesday of the 20th week of Ordinary time, Year One," which happens every other year in mid-August.

I had wondered as I was getting ready that morning whether one of the day's readings might have a secret message for me from God, since I had come all this way for enlightenment. I was not disappointed. The Gospel passage and the sermon that followed seemed intended just for me. The reading was from Matthew 19 and began with Jesus's words: "I assure you, only with difficulty will a rich man enter into the kingdom of God. I repeat what I said: it is easier for a camel to pass through a needle's eye than for a rich man to enter the kingdom of God."

It is a passage I had heard many times before, but never

in a city where the distance between the rich and poor was so dramatic and obvious. I looked across the chapel at women who had voluntarily taken a vow of poverty, and I felt ashamed. At a material level, the contrast of my life of comfort and ease with their simple, unencumbered lives could not have been clearer. At the spiritual level, too, I was the rich man of the Gospel: I was focused on worldly achievement and material things. I was far from heaven, and the humble nuns made this impossible to ignore.

The priest said there are two types of people in the world: those who gather and those who give. And every man must decide which he will be. The nuns around me had all made their choices. But what choice had I made? Nearly all my activities were dedicated to my professional and social advancement—those not dedicated to my own pleasure, of course. Outside of work, most of my time was spent watching television or going to movies and sporting events. I looked around the chapel and saw people my age from all around the world who had come to India to serve others in the most difficult conditions. And there I was, seated among them as a spectator. I was the gatherer incarnate. The priest's homily and the nuns' quiet example also forced me to confront how selfish my trip was; thanks to me, Mother Teresa was about to become a particularly good story to impress Hill staffers at two-for-one happy hours.

The shame of this realization alone would have been enough to transform a humble man. I was ashamed, but equally unbowed. I may have been no selfless servant like the others in the chapel, I thought, but I had plenty of company out in the real world. If I wasn't doing much hands-on work for others, I wasn't harming anyone either. The priest demanded a choice, but I was sure I could be a gatherer *and* a giver.

Shortly after the homily, I caught my first glimpse of Mother Teresa as she walked up to receive Holy Communion and distribute it to her sisters. It was only for a moment, then the congregants stood, and she was lost again in a sea of white saris. The sisters filed out of the chapel in a rush. They and the other volunteers were off to do their work in the Missionaries of Charity's homes: caring for the infants at the Shishu Bhavan orphanage, tending to the dying at Kalighat, or bathing and feeding the disabled or mentally ill at Prem Dan. These givers were alive with purpose; they had somewhere to be.

This tourist, on the other hand, was in no rush. I had come to Calcutta to gather, not give, and it seemed the nuns were doing a fine job without me. I was soon alone in the chapel. I had spotted Mother Teresa again as she filed out with the others but did not know where she had gone, and I had the impression I was going to have to hunt her down. But, within moments, she re-entered the chapel to do her daily meditations on the passion of Christ as represented in fourteen images—what Catholics call the Stations of the Cross—which were evenly spaced along the chapel's back wall. I remained on my bench in the corner as she progressed from one to the next, slowly moving in my direction, holding her small prayer book tightly, inaudibly reciting the prayers appropriate for each station. I was seated below the last one. She finally made her way to the end and stood directly in front of me, only a couple of feet away. She never removed her eyes from the image above my head. She seemed lost in prayer, alone with God.

When she finished this last meditation, she turned and walked over to the front of the chapel to kneel before the statue of Mary, the mother of Jesus. Then she left. I cautiously followed and watched her disappear behind the translucent white curtain that separated the sisters' private quarters from the public areas of the motherhouse. I found a sister nearby, presented my letter of introduction from Senator Hatfield, and impressed upon her how important I was and why I merited an audience with Mother Teresa. She politely asked me to be seated on a bench and went behind the curtain.

Within minutes, Mother Teresa appeared. She burst into the area where I was seated with the energy of a schoolgirl. She came out so fast and seated herself next to me so quickly that I didn't have the chance to stand and properly greet her. There I was, sitting next to a living saint! She was so tiny— not even five feet tall—but had large soft hands that enfolded mine when she welcomed me. They were like pillows. Her accented English was perfectly clear. Her hazel eyes locked on mine.

In an instant, I realized that she was everything I wasn't. She was focused, purposeful, cheerful—I was struck by how fully alive she seemed. That week she had turned seventy-five, yet she was youthful and vigorous. She asked about Senator Hatfield and thanked me for his letter. She also asked if I knew her Missionaries of Charity sisters in Washington. I confessed to her that I didn't, and she asked me to convey her greetings to them upon my return.

Then came her fateful question: Had I been to her Home

for the Dying, Kalighat? I explained that I had only arrived the day before, though a simple no would have sufficed. "Go there," she said, "and ask for Sister Luke." I told her I would be pleased to go to Kalighat. I had the rest of the day to kill, and I thought the visit might lead to the kind of wondrous experience that Malcolm Muggeridge had described in his book. Even if it didn't, it would no doubt make for a good story for the folks back home.

This concluded our brief conversation—it lasted only a few minutes. She stood up and, Indian-style, clasped her hands together in front of her face to bid me goodbye. She turned and was gone.

From an early age, Agnes Gonxha dreamed of a missionary's life. She knew it would be a life of hardship and austerity. But she did not want an easy life, and her early experiences as a nun did not disappoint. In 1931, the newly professed Sister Teresa was sent to the Entally neighborhood of Calcutta, to the walled Loreto compound where about seven hundred Indian girls boarded and studied. Most of the girls attended classes in English at the main school; at Saint Mary's, a separate school also on the grounds, classes were taught in Bengali. Sister Teresa taught history and geography at Saint Mary's and, for a period of time and at her request, was assigned to teach at the local parish school, Saint Teresa's, an experience which introduced her to the misery just outside the compound.

In May 1937, Sister Teresa took her final vows as a nun and received the name "Mother Teresa," following the Loreto custom at the time. She continued teaching at Saint Mary's, but began to take small groups of students to tend to the suffering poor in the sprawling slums directly adjoining the convent property. "Every Sunday I visit the poor in Calcutta's slums," she wrote to a friend back home. "I cannot help them, because I do not have anything, but I go to give them joy. . . . Now I do not wonder that my poor little ones [her students] love their school so much." In one house, twelve families lived together, a tiny room for each. After visiting such homes, she was no longer surprised at so many of the children having tuberculosis. Her heart broke as she saw children who needed much more than a geography teacher.

Not far from Entally, conflict was brewing. Another world war was coming, and tensions were high in the region after Japan's invasion of China. The British Raj was under increasing pressure from Mohandas Gandhi and the other nationalist movements demanding Indian independence. Their cause only gained momentum when, in 1939, the United Kingdom declared war on India's behalf. The declaration fomented further domestic unrest.

As Imperial Japanese forces moved up the Malayan Peninsula in 1942, India, and particularly Bengal, the province of which Calcutta is the capital, came under increasing threat. Even the Loreto compound was on a war footing. Most of the nuns were relocated to safer locations within India or sent home to neutral Ireland. Mother Teresa was one of two who stayed with the student boarders who could not evacuate. Saint Mary's School had been requisitioned as a military hospital, and she rented quarters in two locations for classes and shelter. The workload was unrelenting. She was taking care of three hundred schoolgirls during a war, and it nearly broke her health. She was ordered to take hours of midday rest daily, but still taught seven grades of students, calmed the fears of the hundreds of girls, and arranged their meals.

This last may have been her greatest feat. The 1943 Bengal famine claimed the lives of at least two million people, and displaced untold others. The province faced a vast humanitarian crisis. Squatters from the countryside inundated the city, foraged for food, and fought not against the Japanese but starvation. Mother Teresa and her students could do precious little to mitigate the suffering of the hungry masses streaming into the slums as they struggled to survive themselves.

When the war ended in 1945, Indians demanded an end to colonial rule, though what the major population groups thought independence should look like afterward differed quite widely. Some, like Gandhi, wanted an independent India to remain united and provide safeguards that protected the rights of religious minorities. Others wanted to carve out a separate Muslim state. On August 16, 1946, scarcely a year after the end of World War II, the simmering enmity between Hindus and Muslims boiled over into bloodshed in Calcutta, as a political gathering of Muslims seeking their own homeland spun horribly out of control. It would become known as "The Day of Great Killing," and years later, Mother Teresa could barely discuss it. Gangs of Muslims went on a rampage, ambushing Hindus and killing indiscriminately. Hindus retaliated the following day with similar savagery. Calcutta was seized with reciprocal acts of ethnic cleansing.

Mother Teresa and her hundreds of students huddled behind the walls of the Loreto convent as the riots raged.

By that time, she had become the principal of Saint Mary's School and was de facto superior of the Bengali congregation affiliated with Loreto, the Daughters of Saint Anne. Because she had no food for her boarders, Mother Teresa bravely ventured out, at great risk to herself, to obtain bags of rice from a military unit patrolling the neighborhood. "We were not supposed to go out into the streets," she recalled, "but I went anyway. Then I saw the bodies on the street, stabbed, beaten, lying there in their dried blood." The British soldiers were stunned to see this tiny woman walking toward them in the midst of all the mayhem. She was truly fearless in her vocation.

———

That afternoon my driver picked me up at the hotel and drove me across the city to Kalighat. The road leading to its entrance was so packed with street merchants and foot traffic that the car could barely squeeze through. That it managed to do so was only thanks to an incessant honking of the horn, which both cautioned and threatened passersby.

We pulled up to the Home for the Dying, which rested on the corner of a vast temple dedicated to the Hindu goddess Kali, and I had to make my way through a throng of beggars and tour guides, both looking for money. I walked through the entrance and asked for Sister Luke. She came out within a few moments. She was much bigger than Mother, wore black horn-rimmed glasses, and did not smile. I launched into a proud recounting of my private meeting with Mother Teresa that morning (I already was dropping her name!), and how she had told me to come see Kalighat. Sister Luke listened to me and then said, "Good! Here's some gauze, here's some benzyl benzoate. Go down to bed forty-six and clean the man there. He has scabies."

"Bed forty-six?" I said, as if seeking a clarification. I hadn't come to Kalighat to volunteer! I had come for the tour! I was in a long-sleeved starched white shirt that I had rolled up at the elbows, with dress slacks and hard shoes—a tad over-dressed, given that the sisters were barefoot and the volunteers wore shorts and flip-flops. I had envisioned Sister Luke greeting me and walking me around, after which I was going to give her some money and leave. I would never have come to Kalighat if I had known I would be pressed into service. Worse, because I had just arrived, I couldn't exactly tell her I had another engagement. I frantically tried to think of a way to weasel out of my predicament but found no plausible or polite way to decline her invitation to help. I took what she handed me and was on my way. I was stuck with Mr. Scabies in bed 46.

The truth is, I was too proud to admit to Sister Luke that I didn't want to touch anyone in that wretched place. What was I going to say when I got back to the United States and my mom asked me what I brought back for her? Scabies? There was not one part of me that wanted to go to bed 46 and clean a dying man. I went only because of my enormous pride. I passed through the room almost in a trance, down the narrow passageway between the rows of cots to the far end of the men's ward where bed 46 was situated.

What I found was a man motionless under a blanket, with sunken cheeks and eyelids barely cracked. He looked dead. I proceeded to sit down on the cot—and sat directly on top of his leg! He gasped. I hadn't seen his leg at all; it was too thin to be perceptible beneath the blanket. He grimaced but was too weak to cry. I quickly repositioned myself, and then just sat there. I had no idea what to do. After a few minutes, a man walked by, one of the volunteers. I said to him, "Sister Luke told me to clean this man. She said he has scabies."

The man responded with a distinct Irish brogue. "That's right, he does."

"What are scabies?" I asked.

"They burrow into the skin and make you itch. You'll see where they are—red mounds on the skin." He was anxious to move on from me as he was in the middle of caring for another patient.

I pressed him with one more question. "Do you know where his scabies are?"

"They are around his anus," he replied matter-of-factly.

The day was getting better and better! The wisp of a man in bed 46 cooperated as I turned him on his side. He winced as I applied the medication to his rash. He stared straight ahead, resigned to the care of the complete stranger perched on the side of his bed.

When I was finished, I rolled him back to how I'd found him. He never made eye contact with me. I gave him a sip of water from a tin cup on the floor to the left of his head. As I stood next to him, I saw how much effort his shallow breaths cost him. Death seemed already upon him. The men around him weren't in any better shape. This room full of deep suffering seemed horrible to me, but of course, it was perfectly to be expected in a home for the dying. I saw a man in the far corner with a hideously enlarged foot, an ailment that a volunteer later told me was filariasis, often called elephantiasis. The sight was so grotesque that I stopped looking around the room completely. I started focusing on my exit strategy, though I had hardly been there fifteen minutes.

But Sister Luke was not done with me. I was summoned from bed 46 and directed to clean three other men, and then to feed a few others, including one whose eyes were swollen shut and another who noted the shocking difference between my healthy forearm and his pitifully skinny one. I continued to follow Sister Luke's orders and work in the ward because I could not find an adequate excuse for leaving. I was certainly not enjoying what I was doing, though as the time passed, I became less repulsed by it.

After about forty minutes of volunteering, I felt I could slip out without scandalizing Sister Luke or humiliating myself. I told her I had to leave to prepare for my departure to the United States the next day. She said to me, "One day is not enough." As I walked out the door, I thought to myself, "Actually, Sister, one hour is enough." I was thrilled to leave Kalighat. I went back to my hotel, cracked open a beer, and thanked God I was leaving India the next day.

During my time at Kalighat, I had not heard any angelic choruses, seen any flashes of celestial light, or experienced any spiritual ecstasy. I was preoccupied the whole time with a fear of catching scabies or tuberculosis from the patients and with trying to figure out how to extricate myself at the earliest opportunity. But there was no escaping the fact that I had crossed a barrier of sorts—I had touched desperately poor people. I had strayed far from my comfort zone and survived. I felt somehow more like a man for having over-come my fears and done some bit of good. I had learned in Malcolm Muggeridge's book that Mother spoke of the dying as "Jesus in His distressing disguise." But I had experienced only the distress and felt nothing of the living God's pres-ence. It wasn't a spiritual experience.

I barely slept that night for fear I would miss my early flight. I was headed for the airport by 4:15 a.m. At first, as we drove through the city, I looked out the window at the bod-ies littering the sidewalk—whole families huddled together with nothing but the clothes on their backs. There was not a solitary block we passed that didn't have homeless peo-ple asleep on the pavement. After a while, I stopped looking. I had had enough of Calcutta. Dum Dum Airport seemed tamer than when I arrived, perhaps because my immersion in the city had deadened some of my sensitivities. But I still made a beeline to the check-in desk—a flight cancellation or delay would have been devastating. When the plane took off, it felt like blessed relief to be leaving India.

I had arranged to stop in Hawaii on my way home, and I certainly felt like I had earned it. Hawaii was everything it was supposed to be—white sand, palm trees, fruity drinks—but I was as uncomfortable looking at the sheer beauty of Honolulu as I had been the raw poverty in Calcutta. The paradise that was supposed to be my reward for braving India felt empty. The contrast between the two places was simply too great to reconcile. The plump pineapples decorat-ing the front desk at my fancy hotel were healthier than the people I had left behind on Calcutta's streets. The attendants watering the hotel lawns brought to mind the morning ritual of street people crouching in gutters using rusted tin cans to wash themselves. The women in bikinis tanning on the shore were a far cry from the young mothers dressed in rags, baking on the hot pavement as they begged.

It was all too much for me to process. The luxuries offered at the resort had lost their appeal. While I reclined in a lounge chair by the pool, I thought of the man seven thousand miles away, lying in bed 46. This wasn't how Hawaii was supposed to be. My five days on the islands of Oahu and Maui were spent in a whirlwind of confusion. I felt off balance, unsure of everything. This emotional chaos was the first stirrings of an epiphany. Something had changed inside me while I was in India. I had gone to Calcutta to see Mother Teresa, hoping to be made whole as the blind man was healed by Jesus. She had opened my eyes instead.

CHAPTER 3

To Choose Always the Hardest

If you are humble nothing will touch you, neither praise nor disgrace, because you know what you are.

—*Mother Teresa*

Iwas somewhere over the Pacific on my way back to Washington when I realized that I might be missing Calcutta and that I definitely missed Mother Teresa, though I had only met her briefly. My thoughts kept returning to Kalighat and my short time there. I could not get the vision of all those gaunt faces and fragile bodies out of my mind.

Mother believed that when she looked at the destitute and dying, she was seeing God's actual presence on earth. It took years for me to more deeply grasp how God, the hungry, thirsty, and sick one, had been waiting for me in bed 46, and that when I had touched that dying man, God had touched me back.

This realization likely would have never happened had I not kept my promise to Mother to visit her sisters in Washington and convey her greetings to them. My comfortable routines and the adrenaline of Capitol Hill pulled at me powerfully, but I felt duty-bound to fulfill my pledge. A guy would have to be a real loser not to keep his word to Mother Teresa!

Ten days after I got back I found the Missionaries of Charity convent in Anacostia, the poorest and most violent section of Washington. Sister Manorama, a tiny Indian nun just a bit taller than Mother, welcomed me at the door and was the picture of kindness and good cheer. She and her three sisters were thrilled to hear stories about my trip, my visit with their mother, and my time at Kalighat.

Just as in India, it was a simple invitation from a little nun that trapped me. Sister Manorama asked, "Why don't you come Saturday morning and help us in our soup kitchen?" She must have thought that if I had volunteered at Kalighat then a mealtime shift in Washington wasn't exactly a tall order. Her request was innocent. My acceptance wasn't. I agreed because, just as with Sister Luke, I couldn't figure out how to say no. What excuse did I have? I was planning to sleep in until ten, eat blueberry pancakes at Eastern Market, watch a college football game on TV, and then go barhopping with friends. I didn't have it in me to tell her the truth. So I agreed to come that weekend, silently assuring myself that ladling out a few bowls of soup for some homeless people wouldn't be nearly as bad as scrubbing scabies on a dying man. I resolved that the visit to the soup kitchen would be a "one and done" exercise, just like Calcutta.

Just a few weeks after the massacres of August 1946, Mother Teresa left Calcutta. She was exhausted and in need of rest and quiet prayer. On the train to Darjeeling, in the foothills of the Himalayas, she had a mystical experience. While in prayer she heard Christ's cry from the cross: "I thirst." This message from God set the course of the rest of her life.

She understood this thirst to be Jesus's longing to love and be loved. " 'I thirst' is something much deeper than Jesus saying 'I love you,' " she later explained. "Until you know deep inside that Jesus thirsts for you—you can't begin to know who He wants to be for you. Or who He wants you to be for Him."

For her, the cry was a specific appeal to slake Jesus's thirst through works of mercy among the "poorest of the poor." What she referred to as "the Voice" explicitly told her to go into the "dark holes" of the slums and bring love and dignity to the poor through the work of her own hands.

The Voice left no room for misunderstanding, telling her: "Your vocation is to love and suffer and save souls. . . . You will dress in simple Indian clothes or rather like My Mother dressed—simple and poor."

"The message was quite clear," she explained to her friend Eileen Egan years later. "I was to leave the convent and work with the poor while living among them. It was an order. I knew where I belonged, but I did not know how to get there."

Mother Teresa's experience on the train to Darjeeling bore some resemblance to Mary of Nazareth's at the Annunciation, the moment the angel Gabriel told her she would conceive and give birth to the son of God. Both women were given tasks beyond human comprehension. As Mary chose to trust God's messenger and submit ("I am a servant of the

Lord. Let it be done to me as you say."), so Mother Teresa believed without understanding. "Total surrender and loving trust are twins," she later observed to her sisters. And nothing less than heroic confidence in God would suffice, because her new duties seemed utterly unachievable: How was this tiny European woman to leave behind the security of the convent and venture out into the ghettoes of Calcutta on her own with no money or help?

She confided in Father Celeste Van Exem, one of the Jesuit priests who assisted at the Loreto convent in Entally. In addition to being her spiritual director, Van Exem was well connected in Calcutta and knew what steps she would have to take to leave Loreto and begin her new mission. She would need permission from the archbishop of Calcutta, Ferdinand Perier; her superior in Ireland, Mother Gertrude; and the pope. It would take her almost two years—six months of which were spent in virtual exile at another Loreto school in Asansol, a city 140 miles from Calcutta—to get everyone to agree. Archbishop Perier dragged his feet for nearly a year, until she finally shared with him the details of three visions she had received in Asansol. She described how she saw a "great crowd . . . covered in darkness" imploring her to take care of the poor; Mary had then made a similar appeal, and finally Jesus himself from the cross. The following month, in January 1948, the archbishop finally gave his consent and pledged to help secure Vatican approval. "I am deeply convinced that by withholding my consent, I would hamper the realization, through her, of the will of God," he wrote in his letter to Mother Gertrude.

These impatient years for Mother were also those that

saw India gain its independence. Bengal continued to suffer periodic outbreaks of vicious fighting between Hindus and Muslims, which only intensified after parts of Bengal were carved out of India to create East Pakistan. The heightened violence in Calcutta and the arrival of legions of displaced Hindus from the new Muslim nation only intensified Mother Teresa's desire to relieve the unremitting suffering of the poorest. As she wrote to Mother Gertrude, "If you were in India, if you saw what I have seen for so many years, your heart too would long to make Our Lord better known to the poor who suffer most terrible sufferings and then also eternity in darkness, because there are no nuns to give them a helping hand in their own dark holes. Let me go, dear Mother General," she pleaded.

And eventually, the Loreto order and the Vatican did let her go. She said goodbye to her friends, cried when her students sang Bengali songs at her parting, and with her few belongings, left the comfortable confines of the convent in Entally that for nearly two decades had been her home. She always maintained that this was the hardest step she had to take in her life. It was, she said, "much harder to leave Loreto than to leave my family."

Before she could begin her mission in earnest, she would need some new skills. So Mother went to Patna, three hundred miles away in the neighboring state of Bihar, to get training from the Medical Mission Sisters, a hardworking group that specialized in treating the poor. She received three months of intensive training and became proficient in treating infected wounds, leprous sores, cases of dysentery, and other grave conditions common among street dwellers.

The seasoned missionaries taught her more than nursing. They gave her practical advice that would sustain her as a caregiver to the neediest, insisting that she must provide for herself, too. A missionary needed simple meals full of protein, a daily siesta, and a weekly day off. They also advised her to keep her head coverings to a minimum while working in India's heat and wear clothing that could stand up to the daily washing essential to prevent the spread of infectious disease. This counsel proved invaluable in the creation of the Missionaries of Charity.

Mother Teresa returned to Calcutta and began her work in the Taltala slums of Entally on December 21, 1948, wearing for the first time what became her trademark: a white cotton sari with blue stripes. It was not only a dramatic break from the long black habit and starched head covering she had worn for nearly two decades, but also a statement of solidarity with those she would serve. The cloth was associated with the lowest caste of Indians. To many, Mother Teresa looked like a beggar woman. "It was shocking to see Mother in this sari," recalls Sister Monica, the eighteenth girl to follow Mother Teresa. "Everyone was speechless." Mother did not tell anyone that her decision to wear a simple sari derived from a vision in which Jesus Himself had dictated what she was to wear. Instead, she explained that if she and her sisters wore traditional silk saris, the poor would be too busy begging from them to be served by them.

Mother Teresa faced ridicule from the start. Many of those who heard of her plans to work among the destitute were incredulous. One Calcutta priest said, "She's a mad woman." Another attributed her works to the "wiles of the devil." And her task did seem impossibly hard. In the slums, she met only dirt and misery, poverty and suffering. She described in her journal an "old man lying on the street—not wanted—all alone just sick and dying," and "a very poor woman dying I think of starvation more than TB." But the poor were happy to have her; one family allowed her to use their dirt floor as a blackboard to teach five children from the surrounding hovels. As word spread of a European nun teaching poor children, the five of the first day quickly became forty.

In those difficult days, there were moments she longed for the security of the convent and the company of her friends there. As she wrote in her journal:

> Today I learned a good lesson—the poverty of the poor must be often so hard for them. When I went rounding looking for a home—I walked & walked till my legs & arms ached.—I thought how they must also ache in body and soul looking for home—food—help.—Then the temptation grew strong—the palace buildings of Loreto came rushing into my mind—all the beautiful things & comforts—the people they mix with—in a word everything.—"You have only to say a word and all that will be yours again"—the tempter kept on saying. Of [my] free choice, My God, and out of love for You—I desire to remain and do what ever be Your Holy Will in my regard.—I did not let a single tear come.—Even if I suffer more than now—I still want to do your Holy Will.—This is the dark night of the birth of the

[Missionaries of Charity].—My God give me courage now—this moment—to persevere in following Your call.

She suffered "tortures of loneliness" those first weeks on her own after decades within the community of a convent, but she would not be alone for long. The first young woman to join her sisterhood came the following month. Her name was Subashini Das, a Saint Mary's student who had known Mother Teresa for years. The young girl chose "Sister Agnes" as her religious name, in honor of her foundress's birth name. The next month, Magdalena Gomes, also a former student, came and was given the name "Sister Gertrude" in honor of the Loreto mother general in Dublin who'd granted Mother Teresa permission to leave. Gertrude was as tall as Mother and Agnes were short and was very popular among the students at Saint Mary's. Further, she contacted a former classmate who also joined immediately, becoming Sister Dorothy. Sister Clare, born and raised in the area that was then part of Pakistan (now Bangladesh), soon followed. A Hindu convert, she had a sympathy for the poor that could be traced to when Mother Teresa urged her and her Loreto classmates to share their food with the children of the Moti Jihl slum.

Within a year, Mother Teresa had twelve young women living with her (although two did not stay long). Four of them were young enough to spend their day finishing their high-school studies, while Mother Teresa and the others worked in Moti Jihl or at the nearby Saint Teresa clinic. In the evening, Mother provided theological instruction and spiritual formation to these aspiring missionaries. The untold sacrifices of this first cohort of young girls was rewarded on October 7, 1950, when the Vatican formally recognized the Missionaries of Charity as an official congregation in the archdiocese of Calcutta.

Mother and her young followers hewed to a strict standard of poverty that was mindful of the poor they served and, more profoundly, of the thirst of Jesus on the cross. She instilled in her original group the practices of "choosing not to have," "giving until it hurts," and "praying the work." Such a lifestyle meant that they would voluntarily forgo many of the comforts found in other convents and instead share, to a degree, the deprivation of the families surrounding them. The women slept on thin mats on the bare floor in a room that was scarcely five hundred square feet. The same room served as classroom and refectory by day and dormitory by night.

As the MCs' number grew, so did their need for structure. Mother wanted a rigorous adherence to simplicity and voluntary hardships to ensure that village girls would not join looking for an easier life than they might have had back home. The schedule she devised was followed with military precision and remains unchanged today, more than seventy years later—allowing only the rarest deviations for necessity or very special occasions.

Each day the sisters get up at 4:40 a.m., are in the chapel for morning prayer at 5 a.m., and then do household chores before returning to the chapel for Mass. Breakfast follows, and then the sisters attend to their missionary assignments, returning at midday for prayer, lunch, a thirty-minute siesta, more prayer in the chapel, and then tea together. The sisters follow with an hour of prayer and spiritual reading, their afternoon work with the needy, and then an hour of adorative prayer in the chapel before the dinner bell rings at 7:30. Household chores, bathing, and preparations for the next day's work follow dinner. A half hour of recreation followed by night prayers concludes the day. By 10 p.m., the sisters of the Missionaries of Charity are asleep.

Admission to the MCs is no easier than the life that follows acceptance, and it can take up to a decade. It all starts with a two-week "come and see" visit at one of the MC convents—a brief immersion into religious life. If the young woman chooses to go forward and, equally important, is accepted by the MCs as a candidate, she begins her aspirancy period. For one to two years, she shares in the work of the sisters while receiving spiritual instruction on a deeper prayer life. If both the candidate and the MCs determine she is a good fit for the missionary life, she exchanges her aspirant's white blouse and blue skirt for an all-white sari and begins a two-year novitiate. During this time, she receives, in Mother's words, "intensive spiritual training in theology, Church history and the Scriptures, and especially in the rules and the constitution of our community." After the novitiate, if both parties again concur, the candidate enters the second stage of formation. She takes temporary vows and receives the blue-striped sari worn by all the MC sisters. Thus begins a six-year period of service that culminates in her "tertianship" year. Each tertian has a reduced workload to allow for additional prayer so she can be certain she is called by God to the MC life. At the end of the year of reflection, if she and the MCs are still in accord, she proceeds to permanent vows and, at the Mass of Profession, recites these words:

For the honor and glory of God and moved by a burning desire to quench the infinite thirst of Jesus on the cross for love of souls by consecrating myself more fully to God, that I may follow Jesus more closely in my whole life according to the charism, life and work of our Foundress, Saint Teresa of Calcutta, in a spirit of loving trust, total surrender, and cheerfulness, here and now, in the presence of my Sisters and into your [the superior general's or her designee's] hands, I vow for life chastity, poverty, obedience and whole-hearted and free service to the poorest of the poor according to the Constitutions of the Missionaries of Charity.

Mother Teresa designed this intensive program to inculcate the virtue of humility. For her, humility was the sure path to sanctity. She taught her sisters the practice of self-emptying and surrendering. In a 1975 letter to her sisters, Mother shared her thoughts on how to cultivate humility:

These are a few ways we can practice humility:
To speak as little as possible of oneself.
To mind one's own business.
Not to want to manage other people's affairs.
To avoid curiosity.
To accept contradiction and correction cheerfully.
To pass over the mistakes of others.
To accept insults and injuries.
To accept being slighted, forgotten and disliked.
Not to seek to be specially loved and admired.

To be kind and gentle even under provocation.
Never to stand on one's dignity.
To yield in discussion even though one is right.
To choose always the hardest.

These lines capture the precepts central to Mother's spiritual formation, and many assume they are her words. But she was drawing from a book she loved and returned to throughout her life, Dom Eugene Boylan's *This Tremendous Lover* (1946). The only original line was the very last—"choose always the hardest"—and was advice I heard Mother Teresa repeat often.

There was rarely a moment's rest for Mother and her small group of followers, between their devotions and caring for the poor. They toiled to satisfy their own basic needs, too. The women carried water for bathing and cooking up and down the fifty-six steps to their one-room quarters each day and washed their clothes by hand on the ground floor near the water tank. Sister Monica, who joined in 1952, recalls Mother once joking, "No one has permission to get sick."

The work the sisters performed was based purely on the needs in their community: "In the choice of works, there was neither planning nor preconceived ideas," Mother Teresa once explained. "We started our work as the suffering of the people called us. God showed us what to do." Sister Monica recounted, "Mother was moved by that passage in the Gospel, 'Jesus went about doing good.'" And for the first several years, that is precisely how the Missionaries of Charity spent their days.

Saturday came, and the people lining up for food that September morning were ungrateful. Some arrived drunk or high; others were angry. Many were both. Most of them smelled. The sisters manning the serving line gave each person some of the soup, baked chicken, and salad that they had prepared that morning. And they patiently showed me what to do. I was nervous and fairly certain that if I looked the wrong way at someone, I'd be wearing the soup. A few said "Thank you," but most moved along in silence, gesturing for more of this, less of that. Some cut in line, and others lied when asked if they had already been served. It seemed that no one wanted to be there. They sulked in line like kids with cavities in the waiting room at the dentist.

Sister Manorama walked around the dining area with her apron protecting her white-and-blue sari, refilling empty glasses with more iced tea, smiling and chattering with everyone, trying her best to bring joy to a room steeped in despondency. Every once in a while, a smile cracked one of the weary faces, but for the most part, the men and women seated at the long tables said little, either picked at their food with dissatisfaction or devoured it and left without a word.

After everyone had gone, I helped the sisters clean up and get ready for the next day's service. They carefully saved everything they could—right down to the aluminum foil they had used to cook the chicken. Sister Manorama corrected me when I tried to throw the greasy foil in the trash. When she began to show me how to scrub it clean, I finally balked. I offered to buy the sisters as much Reynolds Wrap as they needed if they couldn't afford it. That wasn't the point, she kindly explained; they were sharing the poverty of those they served.

It was humbling to watch the nuns as they toiled without complaint to feed those who had shown hardly a modicum of gratitude. The sisters had come from the far corners of the globe—India, Guatemala, and America—but they worked as one and never stood still. The ethic of unremitting labor and good cheer that Mother had instilled in the sisters during the first difficult years in Moti Jihl was very much alive in Anacostia. And they did it all with ready smiles, secure in the knowledge they were truly serving God. Their good deeds had as much of an effect on the volunteers like me as on the poor. Mother Teresa once said to me that "joy is a net by which we catch souls." By the time my first shift in the soup kitchen was over, I was happily in their grasp. My Saturday mornings were now theirs.

| CHAPTER 4 |

Spiritual Poverty

We must free ourselves to be filled by God. Even God cannot fill what is full.

—*Mother Teresa*

It took me a while to understand what Mother meant by "Jesus in his distressing disguise," and I have the Missionaries of Charity to thank for the patient instruction. I didn't enjoy my first stint as a soup-kitchen volunteer any more than I liked my brief tour of duty at Kalighat. But I loved how cheerful the sisters were in the midst of the poor they served. I couldn't remember the last time I'd felt the pure joy that shone on their faces as they served these street people as their honored guests. I became a regular volunteer on Saturdays and an errand boy at nights: getting prescriptions filled and groceries purchased. Instead of cruising the bars for my dream girl on the weekends, I was picking up nuns at the airport.

I could feel the sisters setting a new trajectory for my life, and I liked where I was heading. They were making me a better man. They were the best part of my life. They had nothing and yet they were happy. I wanted to be that way, too. At the time, I was living in a basement apartment nine blocks from the U.S. Capitol. I decided to remove the carpet, trade out my big bed for a smaller one, and generally simplify my life. I had a hard time letting go of my television, though, and resolved to pray about it.

It didn't take long to get an answer. I came home one evening in 1986 from work to find my front door broken open and a man standing in my living room, holding my TV in his hands. I backed up to the curb, legs shaking, and watched him walk out of my apartment with the TV, get into his van, and drive off into the night. He also took my Florida State University basketball letterman's ring, some holiday tournament watches, and other memorabilia that I had from my days as equipment manager for the team. It was as if God gave me a crash course in how to rid myself of the material possessions that mattered to me.

Yet this period in my life was almost euphoric. I loved being around the MCs. We shared a common love for Mother Teresa, and the more I was with them, the more I could see her pure, gentle goodness and rich spirituality in them. They were glad to have my help, and I needed their steadying hand as I forged a new life. My zeal to fully integrate the MCs into my world reached such heights that I considered painting the trademark three-stripe blue pattern of their saris around the top of the white walls in my apartment as a constant reminder of Mother. I decided against it because, even in my enamored state, I realized it was silly.

I was teased by my friends, who missed their drinking

buddy. I had swapped "happy hours" in bars for "holy hours" in chapels, and they didn't know what to make of the "new Jim." Some friends and family members wondered if I had lost my mind, and on that point, I could see why: I was suddenly spending my every spare moment with nuns.

As the weeks passed, I derived more satisfaction from helping the MCs than I did from my Senate job, though that, too, allowed me to help the MCs. By dropping Mark Hatfield's name, I was able to get the sisters' convent in Washington, D.C., exempted from taxation in record time, and I convinced the senator to lean on the chief lobbyist for the grocery chains to donate scores of turkeys to the MCs for Thanksgiving meals for the homeless.

With each passing Saturday, I became more comfortable among the soup kitchen's clientele, and by showing up faithfully, I earned the right to ask them questions about their lives and get to know them a little. I wasn't prepared for what they shared. Their tough exteriors were the result of absent fathers, mothers with bad boyfriends, awful schools, relatives in prison, unstable housing, and enough social and racial injustice to be a way of life. They consumed the drugs and alcohol to make this all bearable. I was learning that the man in bed 46 wasn't the only one slowly dying.

This was my first real introduction to what Mother Teresa described as the phenomenon of "spiritual poverty." She was once quoted as saying that in America, and in the West in general, "there is no hunger for bread. But there, people are suffering from terrible loneliness, terrible despair, terrible hatred, feeling unwanted, feeling helpless, feeling hopeless. They have forgotten how to smile, they have forgotten the beauty of human touch. They are forgetting what is human love. They need someone who will understand and respect them."

Mother Teresa opened more homes in the United States than in any country outside of India, and I think spiritual poverty is the reason. She knew that in America, people were hungering for the bread of friendship, thirsting for acceptance and tolerance, and longing to be clothed in the God-given dignity they were promised. Mother Teresa devoted so much of her energies toward combatting material poverty, malnourishment, and disease throughout the world, but she was just as determined to lessen the pain of those who felt unloved, unwanted, and unwelcome. She knew that beyond food, shelter, and clothing every person has the fundamental need to love and be loved. Whether someone was reaching for a bowl of rice or a hand to hold, it was all the same to her—it was the same thirsting Jesus.

The MCs began their work as the West Bengal refugee crisis worsened, and the little medical clinic Mother Teresa and her sisters set up was nearly overrun by the demands of Calcutta's homeless and leprous. One day she found a woman in the streets who had been "half eaten by the rats and ants." It was a seminal experience. "I took her to the hospital," she wrote in her journal, "but they could not do anything for her. . . . From there I went to the municipality and I asked them to give me a place where I could bring these people because on the same day I had found other people dying in the streets." In 1952, after much hectoring, the local governmental authority finally relented. A Muslim health officer offered her the use of a run-down building at the Kali temple that had once served as a guesthouse for Hindu pilgrims. Kali is the Hindu goddess of death and purification, and the temple was known for its funeral rites. It was in this improbable place that Mother Teresa founded the most important Christian mission of the twentieth century. She named it Nirmal Hriday, which means "place of the pure of heart" in Hindi, in honor of Mary, the mother of Jesus. But then as now everyone referred to the mission as "Kalighat."

Kalighat's doors opened in August 1952 to provide "wholehearted and free service to the poorest of the poor." From the start, Mother faced fierce opposition from a Hindu community that wanted nothing to do with her faith or works of mercy. It was a Kali priest who turned the tide of local opinion. He was stricken with end-stage tuberculosis and would curse anyone who drew near. Mother Teresa cared for him the two weeks before he died at Kalighat, and the other priests who visited him saw both her respect for his Hindu faith and the way his rage gave way to calm thanks to her succor. Opposition to Mother at Kalighat died peacefully with him.

The hospice's one hundred beds were quickly filled with emaciated people suffering from every disease and affliction, brought in from the street to receive a mother's care. From a perch near the main entrance, Mother Teresa directed traffic and oversaw treatment in both the men's and women's wards. It was a true test of her management skills. By the end of 1952, Kalighat had admitted 449 people; 226 of them had died, and 165 had been discharged. She kept meticulous handwritten records of every person admitted to the home she called "the treasure house of Calcutta."

"We help them to die with God. We help them to say sorry to God. To make peace with God according to their faith," she said of her patients. Mother was careful to observe the proper funeral protocols for the diverse faiths of the deceased. Some in Kalighat died within moments of arriving in the reception area, but most lived in the home for months as they regained their strength, self-respect, and, ultimately, independence. All were treated with dignity and love; as one dying patient gratefully told Mother Teresa, "I have lived like an animal on the street but I die like an angel, loved and cared for."

As the MCs' work expanded through the 1950s, so did the number of sisters. Mother Teresa was a demanding superior but asked no sacrifice of the sisters that she was not willing to make herself. It was her lifelong practice to be the first in the chapel and the last to bed. She required all who joined her to learn and speak English so that language did not become a source of division in the motherhouse (hundreds of different languages were native to India). Notwithstanding this quest for uniformity, she did adapt some convent practices to the realities of having women from so many diverse regions share a home. For instance, the sisters from Kerala—the southernmost state of India, where Christianity touched down on the subcontinent in apostolic times and from which most of the new Indian MCs hailed—struggled with the West Bengali food of Calcutta. Mother accommodated them by allowing chilis at meals.

Despite such minor modifications, the MCs did not stray from their embrace of voluntary poverty. The sisters received no salary or health benefits, and were allowed to visit their homes just once every ten years, to avoid the expense of travel. The sisters, including Mother, owned very little. A year before her death, as she made out her will, her personal effects were next to nothing: three saris, two sweaters, a pair of beat-up sandals, her crucifix and rosary, her prayer book and Bible, a box of spiritual books and retreat notes, and her metal plate, cup, and eating utensils marked with a red "Mother" to differentiate them from those of the other sisters.

The MCs wasted nothing. They ate only at the convent. While modernization and technological advances were transforming the world, the MCs remained remarkably insulated from them. Someone once suggested that the sisters could be freed up to help more poor people by using washing machines instead of washing their clothes by hand; Mother responded that she had taken a vow of poverty, not efficiency.

While that was surely true, Mother Teresa was nonetheless remarkably efficient in expanding her mission. Archbishop Perier's permission to found the MCs had come with the stipulation that their work must remain within the boundaries of the archdiocese for the first ten years, so the sisters concentrated their efforts in Calcutta and the surrounding environs. Mother opened a health clinic for Muslims, an orphanage, and makeshift schools for children. She operated mobile leprosy clinics throughout the area and ran a special school for the children of lepers. In 1961, she began plans for a whole village for lepers, which would be called Shanti Nagar or "Town of Peace." She wrote, "The conditions under which the leper families live are terrible.—I would like to give them better homes . . . make them know that they too are the loved children of God and so give them something to live for. . . . I want slowly to build like a little town of their own where our lepers could live normal lives."

By the end of the MC's first decade, 119 women had joined Mother Teresa, all but three from India. The sisters began their outreach in other cities, first in the neighboring state of Bihar, an intensely poor region, and then in Delhi, India's capital. In 1965, the MCs numbered more than three hundred, and the first overseas mission was established in Venezuela. By 1975, more than one thousand sisters were stationed in eighty-five missions in fifteen countries, including a homeless shelter and soup kitchen in the Bronx, New York, Mother's first mission in the United States.

With the MCs venturing farther afield, Mother recognized that even the most dedicated sisters would need help with the round-the-clock care of lepers and the dying. She established the MC Brothers in 1963 as a new order of consecrated men who took vows and received spiritual guidance from Mother, and in rare cases attended seminary. They worked with the sisters, helping especially with the most physically taxing jobs, like carrying patients from the street to Kalighat; they also allowed the MCs to reach people in more dangerous neighborhoods. Father Ian Travers-Ball, a Jesuit priest, was the first leader of the brothers. He took the name Brother Andrew and managed the MC's global expansion. Where the sisters went, the brothers often followed.

As the Missionaries of Charity grew, honors and awards began to chase Mother Teresa, first in India and then around the world. In 1973, she was awarded the inaugural Templeton Prize for Progress in Religion, and in 1979, the Nobel

Committee awarded her its highest honor, the Peace Prize. The most meaningful recognition, however, came at Kalighat on February 4, 1986, which Mother described as "the greatest day of my life." Pope John Paul II came to Nirmal Hriday and spent the morning visiting every patient, holding tightly to Mother Teresa's hand as he strode the narrow aisles separating the rows of the dying. He brought a plate of food to five of the patients, and gave an individual blessing and rosary to each of the men and women in the two wards. He was moved by the precious lives the MCs had reclaimed from the gutters: "Nirmal Hriday proclaims the profound dignity of every human person. The loving care which is shown here bears witness to the truth that the worth of a human being is not measured by usefulness or talents, by health or sickness, by age or creed or race. Our human dignity comes from God our Creator. No amount of privation or suffering can remove this dignity, for we are precious in the eyes of God," he said following his visit, as the two future saints stood side by side for the press.

This project of "proclaiming the profound dignity of every human person" was never far from Mother's mind. In her Nobel speech, she took the opportunity to remind all the dignitaries that "our poor people are great people, are very lovable people, they don't need our pity and sympathy, they need our understanding love. They need our respect; they need that we treat them with dignity."

Perhaps it was her keen sense of the primacy of the need to love and be loved that fueled her lifelong effort to confront the plague of loneliness that afflicted the poor and affluent alike. She did not hesitate when asked what the worst disease was that she had seen. In her opinion, it wasn't leprosy: It was loneliness. "People today are hungry for love, for understanding love which is much greater and which is the only answer to loneliness and great poverty," she once declared. She elaborated on this point in the Nobel speech: "When I pick up a person from the street, hungry, I give him a plate of rice, a piece of bread, I have satisfied. I have removed that hunger. But a person that is shut out, that feels unwanted, unloved, terrified, the person that has been thrown out of society—that poverty is so hurtful and so much, and I find that very difficult. Our sisters are working amongst that kind of people in the West."

In October 1985, just ten weeks after I met her in Calcutta, Mother Teresa was to speak to the United Nations General Assembly in New York. I couldn't let the opportunity pass me by to see her again, and using Senator Hatfield's name, I finagled a ticket and took the shuttle to New York. At the time, I was struggling to reconcile my new part-time life with the MCs in Anacostia with my day job in the ornate halls of the Capitol, and her words that evening underscored what she told me years later: "If Jesus puts you in the palace, be all for Jesus in the palace. And if He takes your life and cuts it up into twenty pieces, all of those pieces are His."

I crashed the reception afterward and waited in the receiving line to talk to her again. She didn't seem to remember meeting me, but I didn't care. All that mattered was that I was able to be with her, look into her eyes, feel the warmth of her hands, and hear her voice again.

This second meeting with Mother cemented my decision to help the MCs in any way I could. My timing could not have been better: Mother needed a lawyer to help deal with bureaucratic hurdles as she opened new missions in the United States. The centers would be run by sisters coming from India, all of whom needed visas. Dealing with government bureaucrats was my specialty. The MCs in the Bronx headquarters had already started calling me for assistance after learning I'd helped the sisters in Anacostia with their visas and similar legal matters. I was developing a relationship with the MC hierarchy in New York, and word reached Mother Teresa.

She needed assistance launching an AIDS home in Washington, and here I could help. The D.C. government was not offering the same cooperation she had found in New York. But the mayor's obstinance was my good fortune, for the longer the negotiations dragged on, the more deeply enmeshed I became in the tight-knit MC community. We eventually prevailed, and the Gift of Peace home opened in November 1986, just five miles from the White House. Mother liked that I wasn't just doing white-collar work but also regularly helping the sisters in the soup kitchen and attending holy hours in their chapel and Mass on Saturdays. It was about six months after her speech in New York that she summoned me to Anacostia for a meeting to discuss her upcoming travel. As we sat at a small table in the parlor adjoining the chapel, she wrote on a scrap of notebook paper the names of five countries she wanted to visit. Then she handed me her Indian diplomatic passport and asked me to arrange her visas. I admit I looked at it from time to time in disbelief.

I would have done anything Mother asked, and I was soon put to a far greater test. Gift of Peace needed night-duty volunteers to work from 6 p.m. to 6 a.m. so that the sisters wouldn't burn out trying to provide the round-the-clock care for dying men and women. Mother recommended to Sister Dolores, the home's first superior, that I volunteer one night a week in the men's ward. This work was an order of magnitude beyond anything I had yet been asked to do, even at Kalighat. Scabies is one thing, but Mother Teresa was proposing I help care for people who had an infectious disease with a 100 percent fatality rate at a time when no one knew for certain how it spread. I had to decide: Was I all in or not?

It didn't take long for me to realize that if Mother wanted me to care for people with AIDS in her hospice, then she could count me in. I reasoned that if the MCs weren't afraid of getting AIDS, then I wouldn't be either. This was a turning point for me. It required a leap of faith and some courage to bathe men, change their diapers, and watch them waste away. I had been repulsed just seeing such things a year before in Calcutta, but a lot had changed since then.

I was in good company with the first group of night volunteers at the Gift of Peace. We cared for the men who came to spend their last days with us, starting with our first two patients, Cliff and Andy. Few of the men stayed for more than a few months. Death came to the home regularly, sometimes while I was on duty. It was intense work, but it was beautiful and holy work.

| CHAPTER 5 |

A Born Entrepreneur

Even Jesus could not pick twelve good disciples.

—*Mother Teresa*

Over the next two years, I saw Mother whenever she visited the United States, three or four times total. At first, I continued my job on Capitol Hill, volunteering for the sisters in Anacostia or at the AIDS home at night and on weekends. But the more time I spent with the MCs, the clearer it became that my heart was with them and not Senator Hatfield. So in October 1988, I resigned from my job in his office and became a full-time volunteer for the Missionaries of Charity. I withdrew all the money in my Senate pension fund so I could continue to pay my mom's mortgage and cover my own expenses. I gave away most of my clothes, threw out yearbooks and other mementos, and stored what remained of my worldly possessions in a friend's garage. I felt completely at the disposal of God and dedicated to the life and work of the MCs. This new life gave me numerous opportunities to assist, and engage with, Mother Teresa.

We had already begun a regular correspondence, and I have faithfully kept all her handwritten letters from the Calcutta motherhouse. Her changing salutations reveal the trajectory of the trust and then friendship that began to form between us. In her first letter, in September 1985, she addressed me as "Dear Mr. J. Towey." Fourteen months later it was "Dear James," and four months after that "Dear Jim." By 1989, she was beginning her letters "My dear Jim," and I even have one note addressed to me as "Jimmy."

Each letter or conversation with Mother Teresa during this period of my life made me realize the gulf that existed between her total surrender to God and my own conditional discipleship. I wondered if I was holding something back from God. Thoughts of pursuing the priesthood returned, as that seemed a sure path to the kind of wholehearted acceptance of the divine will that Mother and her sisters lived. Volunteering full-time for the MCs still allowed me the freedom to leave at any time, unlike the sisters, who were committed for life. And women were joining in droves.

The Nobel Prize made Mother Teresa a household name, and her order a global phenomenon. Suddenly, she was opening more than twenty new missions a year, twice as many as before, reaching nearly every corner of the earth. In 1984, the year before I met her, Mother opened her 250th house, and half her missions were outside India. In the last ten years of her life, the MCs added an average of twenty-five new missions a year, the great majority on foreign soil. The number of women joining the MCs was so great that there were 250 in the motherhouse preparing to take vows in 1997.

In addition to the MC Sisters and Brothers, in 1984 Mother Teresa cofounded the MC Fathers with Father Joseph Langford. A young American from California, Father Joseph discovered Mother when he was a seminarian in Rome in 1972. While in a bookstore, he saw her photo on the cover of Malcolm Muggeridge's book, not knowing who she was. "There was goodness in her face, a kindness in her gaze," he later recounted. He paged through the book and instantly knew what he wanted to do with his life. She had stirred in him "a new hope in what was best in mankind, and in myself." He wrote to Mother and began volunteering with the sisters. She attended his first Mass in 1978, and two years later, with her permission, he organized a worldwide group of priests to advance her mission and vision; it would later evolve into the MC Fathers. Mother once told me that no one understood the "I thirst" spirituality like he did.

She saw the need for priestly service as part of the MC mission. In addition to doing hands-on work in the missions, the MC Fathers would help with the sacramental and spiritual needs of both the poor and the sisters. The order began in the Bronx with just two priests—Father Joseph and Father Gary Duckworth—and seminarian Brian Kolodiejchuk, and it remained a small, select group. Like the MC Brothers, who had worked alongside the sisters since 1963, the MC Fathers initially patterned their manner of life and schedule after the sisters but over time found their own distinct identity. The three divisions of the MCs have always worked well together, united by a common purpose and foundress.

Mother's day-to-day life consisted mostly of interactions with an inner circle of sisters and friends. Over the years, this circle expanded or contracted depending on her mission requirements and health condition. Her core support group consisted of the five sisters who were elected to the MC governing council and the senior sisters and MC Fathers with whom she traveled. She also worked closely with a handful of outsiders who had skills or contacts she lacked. In the early years, for example, Dr. Senn was vital to the Missionaries of Charity's care of Calcutta's lepers, and Eileen Egan, a staff member at Catholic Relief Services, facilitated Mother's food distribution efforts.

No one was more indispensable to Mother's navigation of India's intricate internal affairs than the Kumars. Naresh Kumar, the finest Indian tennis player of his generation, was a respected businessman. His wife, Sunita, was a self-taught painter and mother of three, who met Mother in the mid-1960s while assembling medicine packets for lepers. They were instantly friends. On their first visit together to Kalighat, Mother advised Sunita: "Don't think of them as dying. Just smile at them, and they will smile back."

The Kumars' home was the only private residence in Calcutta that Mother Teresa visited with any regularity. When she needed reliable telephone service for a private call to the Vatican, she knocked on their door. When Mother or her sisters were sick, the Kumars made the arrangements with area hospitals and doctors. When Mother was near death in 1989, the Kumars worked the phones to get an emergency visa issued by the Indian consulate in New York City in the middle of the night so an American physician could race to Calcutta. The risky procedure he performed to remove an infected wire from her pacemaker saved her life. When Mother passed away eight years later, Sunita broke the news to the world at a hastily arranged press conference at the mother-house, with Sister Nirmala, Mother's successor, at her side. To this day, she acts as an informal press secretary for the MCs, helping them respond to media inquiries.

As the MCs expanded globally in the 1970s, Mother needed more and new types of help. Sandy McMurtrie met Mother in 1981 when she was trying to put the pieces of her life back together after a painful divorce. She had seen a news item on Mother Teresa and "immediately thought meeting with her would help my children and me through this difficult time and help us emerge closer as a family," she recalls. Her family watched her three children so she could set out for India on a Catholic Relief Services trip with the hope of meeting the diminutive nun. Fate placed the two on the same Hong Kong-to-Calcutta flight—and in the same row, no less. Sandy introduced herself to Mother Teresa in the baggage claim area and was invited to the MC convent the next morning. When she arrived, she was put to work. "Although I was a stranger, she took me in," Sandy recalls. "She started including me in her daily activities, as if we were old friends."

Sandy's month in Calcutta led to sixteen years as Mother Teresa's friend, confidante, benefactor, and frequent travel companion. She was by her side during the 1980s and 1990s when Mother established missions in more than twenty American cities. She accompanied her to meetings with Presidents Ronald Reagan, George H. W. Bush, and Bill Clinton, and she steadied Mother's wheelchair on a makeshift stage in Statuary Hall of the U.S. Capitol when the eighty-seven-year-old nun was awarded Congress's highest honor. Because of her own obligations at home, Sandy seldom traveled with her abroad, but when Mother met for more than two hours with Fidel Castro in Havana, Sandy was there.

This closeness with Mother was rivaled only by that of Jan Petrie, who traveled the globe with Mother and ran interference for her with the media and with religious and civil leaders. Jan, a Canadian, coproduced with her sister Ann the masterful documentary *Mother Teresa*. Mother treated Jan and Sandy like daughters, if not sisters, even granting them access to some private areas within her convents.

The Kumars, Sandy, and Jan alternated as gatekeepers, travel aides, and protectors as Mother increasingly interacted with the secular world in the last two decades of her life. I was granted entrance into her inner circle to provide advice on legal and governmental affairs. It was not a social club— Mother was all business until the very end. Had I met her in 1975 when she had only the Bronx mission in the U.S., instead of a decade later when she was opening numerous AIDS homes and struggling with immigration issues, I would have had little direct contact with her and could never have befriended her.

But one of the things I learned was that Mother Teresa was a born entrepreneur—an aspect of her genius that is usually overlooked. She ran a multinational empire of women doing the most miserable work on the planet for no salary, no benefits, and with no elaborate training. By the time of her death, she had 3,842 sisters, 363 brothers, and 13 fathers operating more than 650 soup kitchens, health clinics, leprosy centers, and shelters for the desperately poor and sick, in 120 countries, at no charge to those served and with no government funds. Mother Teresa attributed her business success to divine providence, and in light of the linguistic, cultural, and religious obstacles she overcame, it's hard to argue. She was clearly created for this purpose. How else could an obscure Albanian teenager grow up to accomplish all of this—and become a universally recognized symbol of God's love on earth?

The rapid growth of the MCs meant Mother needed help with worldly affairs, and I had the honor of regularly solving problems for her. In the twelve years that followed my brief encounter with Mother Teresa in Calcutta, I gradually assumed greater responsibilities as pro bono legal counsel to her in the United States, handling any matters she or her sisters referred to me.

Many years later, I worked for President George W. Bush as director of the White House Office of Faith-Based and Community Initiatives. Whenever the president introduced me at public events, he would invariably joke, "Towey used to be Mother Teresa's lawyer. What kind of a world do we live in when even Mother Teresa had to have a lawyer?" It does seem absurd, but people frequently abused her kindness for profit, and some continue to do so today.

An example: In 1987, Mother traveled to the United States to give a speech at the request of an archbishop. The priest who met her at the airport was as smooth as silk, showing up with a limousine (which Mother refused to ride in). At the event site, they were headed toward the stage when the priest suddenly shunted her into a makeshift portrait studio set up in a side room. He said the photo was simply for the local Catholic newspaper and put a form in front of her to give the archdiocese permission to publish it. She reluctantly signed; she thought it wrong to question a priest unless she had reason to mistrust him.

Mother disliked having her photo taken under any circumstances, and this unexpected portrait session had annoyed her more than usual, so the portrait looked a lot like a mug shot. She gave her speech and left. She thought nothing more of this odd exchange until three years later, when advertisements began to appear in major newspapers throughout the world. One in the *Washington Post* read, "Mother Teresa, one of this world's living treasures has, for the first time ever, authorized her portrait to be reproduced in a special, collector's edition lithographic print." The priest and the photographer had conspired to sell millions of these "authorized" portraits to endow the needs of the archdiocese—starting with a new $200,000 organ—and make a small fortune for two investors. Mother wanted me to put a stop to the scheme. More important, she wanted any dispute with the archbishop resolved quietly: "I forbid anything public. It involves the Church, and I don't want to hurt the Church. You must be careful." We came to an agreement, the terms of which remain confidential, but the pictures were destroyed and the priest apologized for misleading her. She was happy when I telephoned with the good news.

This case and the dozens more like it are why Mother Teresa needed a lawyer. Nor was I the only attorney in her service. The MCs had hundreds of missions around the world by the time I met Mother, and they often had to retain local counsel. They already had a fantastic pro bono lawyer in the United States, Dianne Landi, whose firm handled business and real-estate matters for the MCs. But during the last twelve years of Mother's life, I handled the majority of the legal matters that came her way, whether they pertained to immigration issues for her hundreds of sisters coming to America, government regulations for the missions she was opening, unauthorized fundraising on her behalf by others, or the illicit use of her image or name.

It was this last category that made for the most interesting work. It's rare enough to be a household name around the world, rarer still that the fame is due to something nearly everyone admires. So it will come as no surprise that any number of people and corporations wanted to hitch their wagon to Mother.

Some cases were funny, like the "Mother Teresa Breath Mist," manufactured in Pittsfield, Massachusetts, that promised to "purge the demons of bad breath." The label went on: "Be merciful to thy friends and neighbors . . . deliver yourself from the unGodly scourge of halitosis." Mother had a good laugh, and I put a stop to the breath spray.

Others were forgivable, like the Missouri business selling a "Missionaries of Charity" doll as part of "The Blessings Nun Doll Collection." The figure was draped in Mother Teresa's trademark blue-and-white sari and carried a price tag of $189. The business owners were devout Catholics, and as the doll wasn't named after her, Mother decided to let them keep selling it.

Some companies sought permission to use her name and image in advance, while others sought forgiveness afterward. Samsung Electronics asked Mother Teresa for permission before launching a marketing campaign in South Korea with a photo of her and the caption "Samsung thinks of responsibility to society before its own." Tylenol didn't ask permission before it published an ad that included a photo of Mother Teresa alongside Abraham Lincoln, Benjamin Franklin, and John F. Kennedy, and invited the viewer to "Picture yourself among these leaders." We put a stop to both.

There was nothing to be done about some fraudulent uses of her name. During the Balkan wars in the mid-1990s, the "Humanitarian Organization of Mother Teresa" operated health clinics in Croatia that reportedly performed abortions and used trucks emblazoned with Mother's name to transport both food and smuggled weapons to combatants. The MCs made appeals to the U.S. government and relief organizations, including the International Red Cross, but no one could stop this.

Efforts to use Mother's name didn't cease with her death. In 1998, Steve Jobs wrote an admiring letter to the Missionaries of Charity asking to use Mother's image for Apple's "Think Different" campaign, honoring "the great thinkers and inspirations of the 20th century." He hoped to name her one of Apple's "geniuses" in an ad with the famous photo of a beaming Mother Teresa gazing at an infant she held above her head. He wrote, "It is my hope that our use of Mother Teresa's image will make the light that shines in people's hearts glow even brighter." The MCs wouldn't allow it. They were uncomfortable associating Mother with a secular campaign, particularly one led by a company known for its progressive social stances.

Other organizations had less noble aims. In 1997 an international relief organization, Food for the Poor, tricked the

MC homes in the Caribbean into sending them a wish list of what they needed, and then just before the first Christmas after Mother's death, they published those requests in a direct-mail fundraiser to three hundred thousand people. "With your help, the Missionaries of Charity will have what they need. . . . They need our prayers and support now more than ever," the appeal claimed. Nearly a million dollars had poured into Food for the Poor's coffers before we were able to get this shameless solicitation stopped. The money they raised for themselves was turned over to the MCs.

Mother's interactions with local governments were similarly mixed. She knew New York City mayor Ed Koch fairly well from their many interactions during his three terms as mayor. In fact, when he was recovering from a mild stroke in 1987, she made a house call to check on him—and also hit him up for two reserved parking spaces in front of her AIDS home in Greenwich Village. Just before the New York City Democratic primaries in 1989, Koch sold two run-down buildings in the Bronx, which the city had seized for back taxes, to Mother for one dollar each. She planned to use these properties to accommodate the overflow from her nearby soup kitchen and homeless shelter that the MCs had operated for more than a decade at no cost to the government.

Koch lost his race, and his successor as mayor, David Dinkins, insisted the MCs install, at an additional cost of $25,000, an elevator for the handicapped in one of the buildings. Mother objected, saying, "We don't need an elevator. We can carry anyone who can't climb up the stairs. That money could be used to operate a feeding center in Africa for a year." She sent me to New York to deliver the message.

The New York Office for People with Disabilities would not budge, so Mother decided to return the buildings to the city. She didn't want to embarrass the new mayor or jeopardize her good relationship with city officials, however, so in her letter returning the buildings, she thanked Dinkins: "From the first time I came to New York, everybody in the City, all of the officials, The Police, so many people, have been kindness itself, and I am so grateful to you and to all of the leaders, officials, who have helped us." Despite her efforts at discretion, the *New York Times* caught wind of the controversy and wrote a story with the headline, "Fight City Hall? Nope, Not Even Mother Teresa." The buildings went back to the city.

Even in the worldliest matters—those regarding money—Mother was unmovable when it came to the MCs and the needy. In one particularly complicated dispute, an American woman left $1.2 million in her will to the Missionaries of Charity "for the care and comfort of the very poor and destitute in the United States." She had appointed a priest as her executor, and after her death in 1987, he immediately retained an attorney for the purpose of trying to divert this money to the charities of his own diocese instead. He also diverted $67,000 to himself in salary and expenses. After four years, he had not released a penny to the MCs.

He even solicited the help of the archbishop of Calcutta to get the MCs to renounce their interest in the gift. Mother sent the priest a letter of refusal, asking him to "kindly hand over this bequest to our Sisters in the Bronx so that this money will be put to use according to the donor's intention." Undeterred, the priest shifted strategy and asked for an unspecified share of the bequest, which only hardened Mother's commitment. In her handwritten response, for the first and only time in my years representing her, she brought up, at my request, the possibility of going to court: "I have been advised that if we are unable to resolve this matter promptly, it will be necessary for us to take the matter to court. I hope and pray that we can avoid taking that action."

The priest would not be swayed. He offered to release the funds in exchange for Mother donating $250,000 to the local Catholic Charities organization he led. I telephoned Mother in Albania and briefed her. Despite his demand for ransom, Mother refused to bring scandal to the Church by going to court. She appealed to the diocesan bishop instead, writing, "Never in 41 years in the Church have the Missionaries of Charity ever been forced to pay money—by a consecrated priest—in order to get money lawfully ours." We even met with an American cardinal, hoping to solve the problem within the church hierarchy. But within months, the cardinal's attorney let me know that His Eminence was not in a position to intervene, and worse, that the priest was willing to go to court to get some share of the estate proceeds.

In a last-ditch effort to end the conflict privately, Mother asked me to arrange a meeting for the two of us with the priest and his lawyer during the summer of 1992 when she was to be in Baltimore opening an AIDS home. Just after they arrived at the meeting, Mother decided she wanted to talk with the two of them alone. "Better you stay in the chapel and pray while Mother handles this," she told me. I felt I was letting her walk into a lion's den alone, but she didn't need my help.

A half an hour later, the three of them walked out of the parlor and said their goodbyes amicably. "There, finished," she said. "They agreed that we can keep all the money." I was shocked, and asked her how she did it. All she said in response was "Thank God."

CHAPTER 6

A Calling

What I can do, you cannot do. What you can do, I cannot do. But together we can do something beautiful for God.

—*Mother Teresa*

Mother Teresa was a woman in love. Jesus was her all. But the degree to which she depended upon his mother Mary's intercession from heaven cannot be overstated. The theological foundation of Mother's Marian devotion was simple: "No Mary, no Jesus." The MC's founding documents are likewise unequivocal: "Without Our Lady we cannot stand."

Like many good Catholic women before and since, Mother modeled her life after Mary. But few if any have succeeded in being so much like the Blessed Mother. Like Mary, she was born to be a virgin and a mother. Though she had no children of her own, her maternity extended throughout the world. It began with the Missionaries of Charity, spread to her beloved poor, touched those fortunate to work with her, and even reached the many who knew of her only through the press.

"My Sisters, Father, are the gift of God to me, they are sacred to me—each one of them," she wrote to one of her spiritual directors. "That is why I love them—more than I love myself. They are a very great part of my life." When Mother and I would drive up to one of her missions, nuns would stream out, squealing with delight. She would greet each sister as a uniquely beloved child, looking into her eyes and holding her face as she imparted her blessing. I recall dropping Mother off at 10 p.m. at a convent in Mexico after a long day. She was exhausted yet couldn't wait to see her sisters. As I escorted her to the door, I saw a long line of them inside waiting for their mother. They each wanted to be alone with her, and she delighted in their company. Sleep could wait.

And it usually did. She never complained about how little sleep she had, though she woke before 5 a.m. like her sisters and was seldom in bed before midnight. I often saw her vigorously rubbing her eyes to keep them open, but I never witnessed any grumpiness because of sleep deprivation. She demanded cheerfulness of her sisters, and she led by example.

Life as a nun came naturally to Mother. From the day she arrived in India, she never doubted or looked back. Even when still at the Loreto convent, she was renowned for her work ethic, allowing herself almost no downtime. She believed that if the pregnant mother of God could saddle a donkey and go in haste to a faraway place to assist her cousin Elizabeth, then she should have the same sense of urgency in dealing with those suffering in the nearby slums.

For the poor and unwanted, Mother's love was limitless. Sister Clare told the story of a foundling Mother cared for: "We found a boy eaten by black ants and thrown into a dustbin—a newborn." The baby was alive, but there was nowhere to take him, so the sisters brought him to live with them. He had very dark skin, and Mother called him "Kalo Bhaluk," a Bengali diminutive meaning "black bear." After a day at Kalighat, she loved to return home and hold him. She would take care of the day's last business with the baby in one arm.

Mother Teresa made sure her sisters treated one another with kindness. Once, when Sister Monica admitted to Mother she had wronged another sister, Mother told her to apologize. Monica dutifully went, but found the sister asleep. Thinking she was off the hook, Monica happily reported back to Mother, who insisted, "Wake her up gently and apologize."

Just like a mother, she fussed over her sisters and friends. Once, when we were in Mexico together, she noticed I had not eaten lunch. And despite my insistence that I would eat later, she went to the kitchen, spread some peanut butter on two slices of bread, and said, "There, like that. Now you eat this." She then stuffed three bananas into my jacket pocket over my protests, which she thought was very funny. Another time, we happened to be together on Fat Tuesday, the day before Lent begins, and Mother insisted I celebrate with a cup of coffee (we were with the MC Fathers, who usually serve only tea). She suggested I have sugar in it; "it is too dark," she said. She put a muffin on my plate, and then half a grapefruit, and watched me till I ate it all.

Her motherly heart suffered when her children suffered. She would sit at the bedside of sick sisters, applying cool compresses to combat high malarial fevers and giving them the comfort of a mother's touch. Sister Leonia was bitten by a dog and contracted rabies. Her sisters observed her having spasms and making barking sounds, classic signs of this dreaded, incurable disease. Mother remained by her side for the last forty-eight agonizing hours of her life.

Mother had a vast spiritual family, and her heart was pierced by the departure from this earth of those she loved. She grieved the death in 1993 of Father Celeste Van Exem, her spiritual guide in the years when she was leaving Loreto and the man considered by some to be cofounder of the MCs. Then Sister Agnes, the first girl to join the MCs, in 1949, died just five months before Mother in 1997. Mother called Agnes her "second self" and could hardly bear such grief.

Sister Sylvia, who was very close to Mother and oversaw MC homes in the United States, was traveling with Sister Kateri when defective tires on their passenger van exploded on an interstate highway near Washington in 1995. Both died in the accident. I was told by an MC sister who was in Calcutta that evening that at the moment of the fatal crash, Mother Teresa awakened in the motherhouse and asked the sisters in the next room, "Who is crying? I hear a sister crying."

Mother's faith in God's providence carried her through this and countless other tragedies, including personal ones, such as separation from her family. Her mother and older sister were living in Albania when it fell under the merciless rule of the Communist dictator Enver Hoxha in 1946. They were trapped behind the Iron Curtain. Mail had to be smuggled in and out of the country, and Mother did not have any news of her family for eleven years. When she finally received word in 1957, Mother Teresa wrote a friend: "I had a long letter from my old mother. At last they received news of me—and it is only now that she knows about the Missionaries of Charity. In 1948 she heard I was leaving Loreto—and then nothing—so she thought I was dead." This period of silence had been excruciating for both of them.

Her mother wrote to her, "I want to see you before I die. This is the only grace I ask of God." Mother Teresa resolved to fulfill this wish. In 1965, she went to the Albanian embassy in Rome to beg for permission for her mother and sister to leave the country. She said to the Albanian official that "I came as a child seeking for its mother. Then I explained that my mother is old and ill. She is eighty-one and longs to see me as I long to see her after so many years. I told him that I was helpless to do anything, and that only the Albanians could give her the permission to come to Rome."

Though the official was moved to tears by this desperate appeal, his government denied the request. Mother Teresa took the bad news with her characteristic trust in God, but she did not deny the emotional toll it exacted. "You don't know what this sacrifice of not seeing my mother has obtained for my Sisters," she later wrote. "Her and my sacrifice will bring us closer to God."

Mother Teresa received word in July 1972 that her mother had passed away. Her sister, Age, died a year later. After the dictator Hoxha's death in 1985, Mother Teresa was finally able to travel to Albania and had her mother's mortal remains reinterred next to Age's. They would await eternity side by side. Mother placed a crucifix on each gravesite and then kissed their tombs.

Fortunately, her brother Lazar had moved to Italy before the Iron Curtain fell, and when Mother began traveling abroad, she was able to visit him and his family. His daughter, Agi Guttadauro, had grown up on stories from her father about his little sister Agnes: how she had smuggled him food when he was sent to bed without dinner for misbehaving, and sometimes even did his homework for him. Agi was the closest Mother Teresa would come to having a biological daughter. Mother visited them whenever she could in Italy, relishing their time together. It was a great sacrifice for Mother to forgo having her own family. But she was mother to her sisters and to her friends, including me. And she helped her spiritual children discern their vocations, be they in religious life or not, and surrender totally, as she did, to the will of God.

It was a hard life, and not all who loved it were called to be sisters.

In 1987, my future wife, Mary Sarah Griffith, put her studies at Davidson College on hold and went to Calcutta in search of Mother Teresa and a direction for her life—just as I had done two years before. Desperate to fill a gnawing spiritual emptiness, she had decided to spend the winter in Calcutta, serving and praying alongside Mother Teresa and her sisters.

She arrived after the YWCA hostel was locked for the night, so she slept on the pavement her first night in Calcutta. For the next two months, she labored in quiet obscurity in the MC missions, beginning and ending her days in the motherhouse chapel where she often sat near Mother Teresa. She never introduced herself, but she studied Mother intently.

Mary returned home to the suburbs of Washington, D.C., convinced that God was calling her to be a nun. She contacted the MC house in the Bronx, and Sister Frederick welcomed her news. She instructed Mary to spend time in the Gift of Peace AIDS home, which had just opened in D.C., and to work and pray with the sisters until the following May when new candidates would be admitted. Mary became a live-in volunteer at Gift of Peace, and it was there that I first saw her, mop in hand, swabbing the floor.

From the sisters, I learned of Mary's plan to enter the MCs, and I admired her for it. Once in a while I ran into her in the volunteer kitchen when I did night duty with the men upstairs, but we didn't chat. There was always a rush to get to the residents and begin putting them down for the night, and besides, small talk was discouraged with sisters and women like Mary who were waiting in the wings. Young men who were not priests were not often granted access to Mother or her sisters. I was very careful to maintain a safe distance from the women.

I couldn't help but pay more attention to Mary after seeing her laugh. About a month before she was to enter the convent in the Bronx, the sisters decided to entertain the Gift of Peace residents with a short play about the 1858 appearance of the Virgin Mary to the fourteen-year-old Bernadette Soubirous in Lourdes, France. The sisters tapped Mary to direct and assigned two residents, Nila and Debbie, to star in the production. Like all the residents, they both suffered from AIDS. They had been drug addicts and prostitutes, and had survived great hardship, but the love of the sisters at Gift of Peace was slowly softening their sharp edges. Nila was to play the Blessed Mother and Debbie the young Bernadette.

On the day of the play, the residents assembled, about twenty-five in all, and the walls were lined with sisters and volunteers who had come to enjoy the show. Mary looked beautiful, director's notes in hand, in a pink sweater and floral print skirt. She welcomed everyone and read the introduction to the play. Debbie picked imaginary flowers as Nila appeared in the makeshift grotto, with her head covered by a blue veil and halo. Debbie recited the first line just as rehearsed: "What is your name?" Nila was supposed to respond just as the Blessed Virgin had in 1858, "I am the Immaculate Conception." Instead, she said, "Hi, I'm Nila."

Debbie shot back, "You dumb bitch. You were supposed to say, 'I am the Immaculate Conception.'" The audience gasped. The argument between the two quickly became more heated. Mary Griffith covered her face and started to laugh. I did just the same thing. It was unforgettable.

A few days before Mary left for the Bronx, we had a farewell dinner at a Thai restaurant. It was my idea and innocent enough because we both were intent on giving our lives completely to God and no one else. She told me how she believed God was calling her to the religious life as a nun, and I shared that I was seriously considering the priesthood. It was a spiritual date, and nothing more. Before she left for good, she sent me a copy of another Malcolm Muggeridge book, *Jesus Rediscovered*.

Mary Griffith became Sister Katrina in June 1988 and disappeared into MC convent life. Five months later, I quit my job in Senator Hatfield's office and went to live with the MC Fathers in their seminary in Tijuana, a place Mother Teresa described as "one big city of poverty." Father Joseph took me under his wing as I worked full-time for Mother. My life in Mexico was much like the one Mary had in the Bronx. The schedule was regimented and provided ample time for prayer and work but little for rest. The needs of families in the *barrio* where the fathers lived were immense. When I wasn't packing *dispensas*, the bags of food staples that we handed out twice a week, or visiting the families' simple homes, I was working on projects that Mother Teresa or Father Joseph assigned me. He and I talked for hours at a time about vocational discernment, prayer, and MC spirituality. We also compared notes on the recent election of George H. W. Bush and what that might mean for our native country.

I traveled frequently with Mother during my year with the MC Fathers. In June 1989, I accompanied her to Memphis, where she opened a new home, and then on to Washington, D.C. I was waiting for Mother in the common room of Gift of Peace when Mary Griffith walked through the front door. I was startled: She was not in the white sari she would have worn as an MC postulant, but in ordinary clothes. She sat down next to me, and I asked why she was back in Washington. She explained that Sister Frederick had told her that she wasn't called to an MC vocation, and she had come to appeal this decision directly to Mother Teresa. Within moments, Mother appeared and took Mary by the hand for a closed-door meeting in the parlor. Ten minutes later, Mary came out, tears streaming down her face, and departed without so much as a glance in my direction.

I didn't find out what had happened until I was back in Mexico. I got a rare phone call on a Sunday afternoon from another full-time volunteer with the MCs, Ralph Dyer. "Did you hear the news?" he asked breathlessly. "Sister Katrina is out. She's no longer with the sisters." I had suspected as much; Mother would not have overruled Sister Frederick. But there was an ulterior motive to his call: Ralph had never thought I was cut out to be an MC father, or a priest for that matter, and he thought the world of Mary. While he didn't explicitly say I should consider a future with her instead of the MC Fathers, the fact that he was calling made that point quite clear.

I continued on with my year with the fathers, but the fact that Mary was back in society may have interfered with my discernment of a celibate vocation. As much as I loved the thought of being a priest, I didn't feel called by God to be one. In January 1990, I took my leave of the fathers and went to Calcutta to confirm with Mother that this was the right decision and make sure that I wasn't saying no to God. If she had told me to enter the seminary, I would have done so without question, but she didn't. She told me to "pray that He uses you without consulting you" (advice she would give me again and again). Then she said I should bring Jesus to the places where she couldn't go, like the White House.

Sister Priscilla, one of her confidantes in the motherhouse and the congregation's general secretary, told me that Mother had decided to write a letter to President George

H. W. Bush and ask him to give me a job. I wasn't thrilled
with this news. I thought I was finished with political life in
Washington and didn't want to inhale the odorless gas that
intoxicates those around power. Mother seemed adamant, so
I tried to lower her sights a notch. Maybe she could send the
letter instead to John Sununu, Bush's chief of staff, I suggested, "so that the president isn't bothered with this."

The next day, Mother handed me a handwritten letter:

Dear Mr. Sununu:

*I am writing to you concerning Jim Towey whom
I first met in 1985 while he was working for Senator
M. Hatfield. Jim Towey has been helping our Sisters in
Washington D.C. in his free time since 1985 and last
year I invited him to help our MC priests and Sisters in
our Mission at Tijuana close to the border of San Diego.*

*Jim stayed 15 months in Tijuana, helping the MC
Fathers in many ways, bring joy and peace and love to
the poor whom they serve.*

*Now Jim is returning to government work in Wash-
ington with my blessing, and it is my hope that you will
be able to give him a suitable job.*

*My gratitude to you is my prayer for you, your fam-
ily and the people you serve.*

Please pray for me and Our Poor.

God bless you,
M Teresa mc

I left Calcutta with three things: her blessing, the letter,
and typhoid fever. Within days of my arrival in Washington, I

had high fevers and debilitating weakness. I moved into one of the volunteer rooms at the Gift of Peace and was as sick as some of the residents down the hall. Mary had returned to her collegiate studies—this time at Catholic University—but was still volunteering at the AIDS home. Sister Dolores, the superior there, sent Mary upstairs to my room with soup and juice. She knew Mary's soothing presence and wonderful laugh were more medicinal than what she brought on the tray. It would later become clear that Sister Dolores was as intent on arranging a marriage between Mary and me as Ralph. When I recovered and was back to my full-time duties at the Gift of Peace, the sister redoubled her efforts. For instance, she once asked me to take the men on an outing to the zoo, and as I was loading them into the van, Mary arrived to accompany the women on the same outing.

Meanwhile, Senator Hatfield forwarded Mother Teresa's letter to John Sununu, who arranged for me to meet with his deputy, Andy Card. He told me that there were no openings on the White House staff, but they would look for a place for me in the administration. I was not disappointed by his news and not particularly interested in a job in the government. I was happy to be immersed in the lives and needs of the residents at Gift of Peace and in no rush to return to the rat race. Months passed, and no job offer emerged, but Mary and I drew closer in this most unusual of courtships—she living with her parents, and I in an AIDS home.

By the end of the year, however, I had burned through my savings and pension and had to return to gainful employment. I interviewed for a job with the newly elected governor of Florida, Lawton Chiles, for whom I had briefly worked when he was a U.S. senator. I showed up wearing a suit someone had donated to the MCs. He hired me, he said, to be his "eyes and ears with the poor." It was an appealing prospect, and more, he understood I wanted to continue helping Mother Teresa and her sisters whenever called upon.

As I prepared to leave for Tallahassee in November 1990, I wrote Mother Teresa a letter telling her that the White House job she envisioned had never materialized, and she wrote back saying, "Since nothing has come from the White House—may be our Lord does not want you to be there." But I also shared my intention of proposing to Mary and asked her approval and blessing. Her handwritten response not only granted me both, but suggested the date on which we should be married. Mary, meanwhile, was finishing her studies in Washington and continuing to help out at the Gift of Peace. Our relationship deepened with every phone call and letter, and I became increasingly convinced that she was the one for me. She had already made up her mind that we were to be married and not so subtly suggested dates and places where we could meet up and become engaged. Her Spanish studies took her to Mexico City in 1991, and I visited her there, disguising my intention to propose by saying that I had come to reconnect with the MC Fathers. We went to Mass at the Basilica of Our Lady of Guadalupe, the most visited Marian shrine in the world. Father Joseph arranged for us to be in a private chapel upstairs overlooking the Mass being celebrated at the main altar below.

At the moment in the service when the priest invites worshippers to offer each other "a sign of peace," I got down on one knee and asked Mary to be my wife. I thought perhaps if

I proposed to her in this sacred space, during a Mass, I might be given special graces and protections to not mess up the marriage. My sweet Mary spontaneously got down on her knees and with tears in her eyes said yes.

In the MC world, our engagement was big news. In a phone call from Albania after I had proposed, Mother told me playfully, "Very good. Very good. You can have your honeymoon in Albania." (This was possibly the only bit of her advice we didn't take.) Mother did make one thing clear, however: "You must have a normal house with nice things that are appropriate to your position. You are not an MC and not to live MC life. You must be normal. You have to provide for your family with a proper job. God will show you what to do."

Mother Teresa came to Washington in December, and we handed her our very first wedding invitation. She kissed and blessed our rings, then held Mary's hands and looked in her eyes, saying, "Even though Mother will be far away, I'll always be with you in my prayers." She told us to have five children—one for each of the joyful mysteries of the rosary. She was already scheduled to be in Mexico on February 1, our wedding date, but she gave rare permission for thirty-five of her sisters to attend our wedding to represent her on our big day.

I had the grace of speaking to Mother Teresa by phone that morning, and when I told her the wedding was at noon, she promised, "I will be in the chapel making a holy hour for you and Mary during that time." All who attended the wedding remembered the sisters' angelic singing, and how Sister Dolores interrupted our triumphant procession down the aisle to place garlands of flowers around our necks.

We wasted no time following Mother's orders to have a big family. Mary conceived within seven weeks of our wedding. James was born at the end of December; Joseph followed twenty-three months later, and Maximilian twenty-one months after Joe (and ten months after an early second-trimester miscarriage that sent Mary to the emergency room).

During those first five years of our marriage, whenever I telephoned Mother on legal matters, she would unfailingly ask about the children. Each time she was with them, she delighted in them. When Joe attended a meeting with me, she picked his pacifier up off the floor and popped it back in his mouth. Each of the baby boys made his own indelible impression on Mother: Jamie bit her, Joe head-butted her, and Max ate the Miraculous Medal she gave him (I had to fish it out of his mouth with my finger). During those years, I made her laugh by always ending our calls with greetings from the boys to their "Grandmother Teresa."

CHAPTER 7

Mother of Outcasts

The biggest disease is not leprosy or TB. It is loneliness. It is being rejected. It is forgetting joy, love and the human touch.

—*Mother Teresa*

I spent the early 1990s trying to balance the demands of a growing family, the many requests for help from Calcutta, and my day job leading Miami's Health and Rehabilitative Services Agency with its five thousand employees. My office was across the street from the police station in the Overtown neighborhood. I was at the center of the brokenness of the city and in regular contact with legions of foster children, the developmentally disabled or mentally ill in state institutions, and the city's numerous impoverished who depended on federal food stamps to survive. Nine months into the job, Hurricane Andrew roared through South Florida and vastly increased the number of beleaguered Miamians turning to the state for help. The work was rewarding and exhausting in equal measure.

I was eighteen months in Miami and then went to Tallahassee to head the entire state's social services network. It was there I learned the limits of what taxpayer-funded programs can do for the neediest. A drug addict or a homeless mother needs more than services from bureaucrats, no matter how well intentioned or guided. The poor cry out for human connection, for someone to care about them. Government can't provide this because government can't love. This is why faith-based and community organizations are often so effective in repairing the broken lives of those they serve. Mother Teresa taught me that the deepest wounds of humanity could best be healed by love and compassion, one person at a time.

The Missionaries of Charity's vow to provide "wholehearted and free service to the poorest of the poor" means not simply working *in* the slums but working *with* the most miserable of the slum dwellers. Take Calcutta's lepers. The disease of leprosy has been with civilization since the beginning. To be a leper has always meant ejection from all organized parts of society, including family and friends, and life in exile as a beggar. In Europe in the Middle Ages, lepers were required to wear special clothing and ring a bell when approaching the unwary. A thousand years later in postwar Calcutta, the stigma of the disease was no less humiliating. They were ostracized and forsaken by all. Mother Teresa's earliest forays into the slums of Entally brought her into direct contact with these overlooked souls. It was such people Mother sought out in founding the MCs. She was unafraid and certain of the solace her mission would bring.

Mother and her Missionaries of Charity set up mobile clinics to bring medical services to neighborhoods with high concentrations of lepers. Mother knew they would be unwilling or unable to travel to a brick-and-mortar doctor's office. By the time I came to witness such work, the MCs had already logged four million patient visits by lepers at such clinics throughout India. Mother also founded Shanti Nagar, a town for lepers and their families about two hundred miles from Calcutta. It was on those grounds that the cotton saris worn by the MCs were woven on looms operated by lepers. Mother spoke proudly of this connection whenever asked about her attire. She sought to give lepers meaningful work and purpose in serving others, instead of simple charity.

Mother's care for all the outcasts was inspired by the example of Jesus. The Gospels record his healing of lepers, his tenderness toward the Samaritan woman at the well and the adulteress thrown at his feet, and the parable of the Good Samaritan. Jesus said, "Come to me, all you who are weary and find life burdensome," and so Mother opened homes reserved for lepers, orphaned children, the severely disabled, and women and girls enslaved in the sex trade.

The outcasts of society brought out the mother in Mother. In her speech at the United Nations in 1985, she alluded to the AIDS home she was opening in Greenwich Village. The world was just discovering the illness that spread terrifyingly quickly through communities of outsiders: gay men and drug users. The disease was so awful and mysterious that those who had AIDS were often left with nowhere to go. People were afraid of these new lepers, and Mother rushed to fill the void. The AIDS home in New York was her first in the United States. Within the next few years, she opened additional such homes in Washington, D.C., San Francisco, Denver, Atlanta, and Baltimore. My time as a volunteer at the Gift of Peace home in Washington was one of great fortune for me; the dying I met showed me courage and unbridled dignity.

Christine and Gregory are two I can't forget. They moved into Gift of Peace in D.C. within months of each other in 1990, and each seemed among the unlikeliest of candidates to have AIDS and be homeless. Both were intelligent and college educated, and each had once held a well-paying job—she with Blue Cross Blue Shield and he with Amtrak. Chris had the manner and face of a fashion model, and Greg had a wit and charm that drew others to seek his company. With all of this going for them, how did the two end up at Gift of Peace?

For Greg, the short answer was drugs. He came from a big family: an older sister, Anita; two younger brothers, Neil and Adrian; and baby sister Bonnie. Their home life had been utterly upended by the murder of their father. Their mother had to work full-time to support the family and that left the teenagers on their own. His brothers quickly turned to drugs, but Greg resisted the pull. Anita's good example gave him the strength to resist, he told me. But one day he saw her secretly using drugs, and he caved. He was quickly addicted, and the drug addict's lifestyle is what eventually landed him on the streets and then in an AIDS home. On the rare occasions when his brothers came to visit, they offered little love or compassion. I once saw them arguing in front of him over who would get to keep his television after he died. They spent his monthly government checks and ignored Greg's requests to bring him a pack of Newports (his preferred brand of cigarettes) and some juice to drink.

Some weeks prior to his passing, I was talking with him and asked him if he believed in God and regretted his sins. He answered in his characteristically blunt way, "Jim, I have experienced everything you can experience in life and look at where it has gotten me. I want to experience God. I think it would be a good thing." It was as simple as that to him, and he asked to be baptized. The sisters made the arrangements and invited his family to attend. I carried Greg in my arms from his room, down the stairs, and into the chapel, where his whole family was assembled. They likely thought he had been coerced and that this ritual was the quid pro quo for his free care from the sisters. It was anything but that. When Father Ryan began the baptism rite by asking "Greg, do you believe in God, the Father Almighty, Creator of heaven and earth?" his response was resounding. Greg's "I do" could not have been stronger or held greater conviction. His mother began to cry and couldn't stop. His siblings were utterly dumbfounded.

From that day on, they became regular visitors and often kept a vigil in his room. On the Saturday before he died, his brother Neil and sister Bonnie came to visit. I was in the room when they arrived, and with an unexpected burst of strength, Greg said, "Neil, come over here, give me a hug." Neil reluctantly obliged with a quick, stiff embrace. Greg looked at him and continued, "You have been a terrible brother, but I forgive you for everything that you have done, and I love you." Neil began to cry. He didn't say a word. He didn't have to.

Christine's downward spiral will forever be wrapped in mystery for me because she had shut down emotionally before arriving at Gift of Peace. She talked little and smiled less. Her only visitor was her grandmother, who came just a few times. Sister Carmel, one of the MCs caring for Chris, knew she was lonely and prepared a birthday celebration for her. The sisters purchased a cake, and we lit a cluster of candles on it. Chris was so weak at this point, I had to remove one of the candles and bring it an inch from her lips for her to have enough breath to blow it out. Even though no friends or family came, she seemed pleased by the party and the attention. One Sunday afternoon, I went out to the parking lot and saw two men swigging from a bottle wrapped in a brown paper bag. I asked them why they were there, and the more drunk of the two identified himself as Chris's father. I escorted him up the stairs to the women's side of the house, where he could see his daughter. The visit was a disaster, I learned later, and only seemed to make Chris even sadder.

She died about a week after her father's visit. Sister Dolores, the superior of the home, announced that there would be a funeral in the larger, upstairs chapel, which was surprising because I didn't think Chris had any family or friends who would care to attend. I was wrong—and shocked. Around one hundred people showed up, packing our chapel. Chris's body rested in a simple coffin in front of the altar, and friends and former coworkers sobbed over it; some even collapsed on top of it in grief. One said loudly, "I am so sorry, Chris, that I didn't come and see you. I feel so guilty." Chris's death seemed to teach them a bitter lesson at a time when AIDS still carried great stigma.

The sisters at Gift of Peace offered Chris and Greg love, care, and forgiveness when their own families and friends couldn't. Greg made peace with his brothers and his past, and Chris's family and friends had a chance to seek forgiveness for their failures. This was Mother Teresa's success. Her life's work sent out ripples of compassion that could transform an AIDS hospice into a place of healing, reconciliation, and acceptance.

Such love was something the state simply could not provide. In fact, it seemed many bureaucrats could not even understand it. The California Department of Social Services tried to shut down Mother's AIDS home in San Francisco in 1995, in large part because of the religious trappings of the care the sisters provided. In its first five years of operation, Gift of Love had been the final earthly home of 134 men. Many of the patients came from San Quentin and other prisons. The sisters loved them all and cared for them, and never asked for a penny from the state, local, or federal governments.

Then in May 1995, the state government notified the MCs that in order to continue operating, Gift of Love would have to comply with forty-four pages of regulations governing "Residential Care Facilities for the Chronically Ill." The new training and paperwork obligations were onerous and costly for a simple house run by nuns with help from a band of faithful volunteers. Other requirements were similarly unacceptable. Meals could no longer be brought in by local churches. The sisters and volunteers had to be fingerprinted. Pornography had to be permitted in residents' rooms, and the religious tenor of the house had to be toned down. If the MCs failed to comply with these rules, they would face daily fines for any "deficiencies" and, ultimately, closure.

The MCs could not accede to these demands, and after

months of negotiation, I could see the state was not going to back down. I finally told Mother we would have to comply or cease operations by the end of the month. Mother Teresa didn't hesitate: "Tell them I will close the home, and to come and get the people." Upon receipt of my letter conveying this decision, the Department of Social Services realized that they faced a humanitarian crisis—and a public-relations disaster. The state suddenly determined "licensure of Gift of Love . . . can be achieved without any major disruption to the facility's operation or services. . . . [We] do not anticipate any major issues that cannot be resolved."

It was not always the state and local authorities standing in the way of the sisters' attempts to care for AIDS victims. The thinly veiled contempt of the general public for gay men, prostitutes, and drug users meant these shelters quickly became the subject of "not in my backyard" resistance. Mother had faced similar opposition in India when she sought to house lepers in locales where residents were appalled by her desire to welcome them. Gift of Peace in Washington, D.C., almost didn't open due to hostility from its neighbors and the D.C. government. The public zoning hearings had been a farce: One neighbor claimed that a mosquito might bite a patient and fly across the street and infect someone. Such fears were common in the mid-1980s, when little was known about AIDS and its transmission. Thanks to a loophole in the zoning regulations, the MCs were able to open Gift of Peace in November 1986 and operate legally. Dr. Anthony Fauci, later of Covid-19 pandemic fame, trained the first group of sisters on infectious disease protocols.

Opposition from the neighborhood only intensified after

the opening, however, and the zoning board threatened to shutter the home. At Mother's request, Senator Hatfield intervened with the mayor, and eighteen months after Gift of Peace had opened, and in the face of continuing local government hostility, Congress took the extraordinary step of exempting the Gift of Peace from D.C. zoning authority. President Reagan's signature made it Public Law 110-462, and the property remains exempt to this day.

It is a sacred place for me, and I thank God it remains open. Nearly all the individuals I cared for at Gift of Peace were adults, but the one who was not was one of the most memorable people I have ever known. In 1987, eight-year-old Tina arrived at the home in an advanced stage of AIDS. She had contracted HIV at birth from her mother, who was a prostitute and addicted to drugs. Her father had already died from AIDS by the time she came to us.

Some months before, Tina had caught the chicken pox. With no parental supervision to protect her from herself, she scratched at her skin until the pox turned into large, open sores. They became infected, and her compromised immune system was powerless to heal them. Where Tina's hands could not reach, the marks had gone away and the skin on her back was as smooth as any child's. But her face, neck, arms, stomach, and legs bore fresh wounds that were infected with *Staphylococcus* bacteria.

These wounds wept blood, and with both AIDS and staph, Tina was highly contagious. The sisters made sure she was bathed every day, which seemed to provide her equal measures of discomfort and relief. All who tended to her had to wear a mask and gloves and exercise extreme caution so as not to become infected through contact with her bodily fluids. Some evenings, she would ask me to remove the tiny fibers of lint that were stuck to her wounds. The lint seemed to distract her from her more serious ailments of incessant coughing, raging fevers, and persistent diarrhea—all common to people with late-stage AIDS.

Tina was in constant pain, yet she almost never complained. She loved to play, even if she was consigned to bed, and had a laugh that made you forget for a moment where she was and why. Her southern accent, bright smile, and loose pigtails won people's love and drew them into her service in spite of her fearsome sores. One Saturday morning, Sandy McMurtrie and her teenage daughters came to clean, dress, and dote on her, and she delighted in their special attention. Sister Dolores took extra care that Tina had just the right amount of company and was neither overexposed nor alone.

I moved into the Gift of Peace to help during the Christmas holidays, which afforded me many hours with Tina. She shared stories of her home life and had no sense of how harsh her childhood had been. She told me how she once found her mother "sleeping" on the floor. Tina brought her a cheese sandwich and glass of milk to try to revive her, never knowing she was passed out. At night, I would often hear Tina's voice echoing through the halls, calling, "Where is my mother? I want my mother!" Once, delirious with fever, she prayed the Our Father out loud in her sleep, repeating some of the lines several times. She would sing "Jesus Loves Me" over and over, indicating that someone somewhere along the line had taken her to church. But usually, she spent her nights tossing and turning, awakening and calling for me to bring her something to drink. She hated being alone. Every so often her beautiful smile and playful brown eyes shone like those of other girls her age. Most of her days, however, were passed in physical torment, weakening by the hour.

Tina lived at Gift of Peace for six weeks. Shortly before she died, Sister Dolores telephoned me in my Capitol Hill office with urgency in her voice: "Tina's mother must come here to visit her daughter before it is too late." Tina's address was on her intake forms, but I knew an unknown man's showing up would likely cause trouble. I contacted a friend I knew from the Hill, Polly Gault, and asked if she would help. Polly was a warrior (she had just been made the executive director of the Presidential Commission on the HIV Epidemic) and didn't fear the neighborhood where she would have to go. Tina's mother—though high and somewhat belligerent when Polly arrived—agreed to come see Tina. On the way to the AIDS home, Polly bought a McDonald's Happy Meal, Tina's favorite, for the mother to give to her little girl.

It was still early evening but dark as night outside when Tina's mother walked into Gift of Peace wearing sunglasses. She was terribly thin, and looked quite sick and frail herself, but projected an air of proud defiance in the face of her humiliation, as everyone knew that she had not been there for her daughter. She ignored us and went right over to Tina, climbed in her bed, and held her like any loving mother would. Amazingly—miraculously—for a moment, nothing could come between her and her little one. She didn't stay long or say much, but she had held her sick child. It was a moment of grace.

I saw Tina the day before she died. She was so weak, her breathing heavily labored. As soon as I walked into her room, I said, "Tina, let's play!" She perked up perceptibly— the child in her was very much alive! She told me to go and get a game for us to play. I left her room in search of one, and when I returned a few moments later, she was fast asleep. It was just as well. Soon she would be at play in eternity, forever young, forever loved.

CHAPTER 8

A Human Heart

Religious have no reason to be sad. Being moody is being proud, thinking only of yourself.

—*Mother Teresa*

"Holiness does not make you less human," wrote Pope Francis in *Gaudete et Exsultate* in 2018, "since it is an encounter between your weakness and the power of God's grace." Catholics believe that grace builds on human nature, which means that saints become saints not by being "super human," but by being fully human—by allowing themselves to be "loved and liberated by God" and "guided by the Holy Spirit."

According to this understanding, Mother Teresa was the most human of women. She shared God's grace with the world through her tremendous maternal love and by her example. She used all her gifts to bring Him glory and complete the tasks He assigned her, and she asked forgiveness for her mistakes and weaknesses. It was not miracles but her humanity and humility that made Mother Teresa so lovable and so exceptional.

In December 1987, I introduced her to my mother, who had come up to Washington from Florida for a visit. Mom didn't mind that I called someone else "mother." Mother Teresa hugged my mom and even insisted on taking a picture with the three of us together. She wanted to make my mom feel special. When I left to live with the MC Fathers, she ordered me to write my mom every two weeks. Mother was good at making people feel her maternal love. She always made sure I was properly fed. She scolded me for rubbing my eyes, saying it wasn't helping my allergies. And I know my family was in her prayers: A sister told me that on Mother's last visit to Washington, in 1997, she had seen a photo of my family in Mother's prayer book, the only family to receive this grace.

Mother put her every talent to work in God's service. Her own mother had instilled in her a love of the arts, particularly music, and Mother had a lovely, low, melodious voice. Whenever we were in the same chapel for Mass, I could always pick out her alto, immediately recognizable from the others and always in natural harmony. Singing seemed to draw her closer to God and her fellow sisters; it was a mainstay of her community life and worship. She had used it to calm her students as hundreds of them hid in the basement of the school at Entally in August 1946. The familiar Bengali songs soothed the girls as the communal violence raged in the city outside.

She was also a gifted writer. She composed the foundational documents of the Missionaries of Charity, as well as scores of letters of instruction that she circulated to her sisters

worldwide. Her style was always plain, and her words were
filled with wisdom. She naturally exposited on scripture with
the insight of a trained theologian. There are thousands of
her personal letters worldwide—always handwritten, usually done late at night. What she said to her sisters, clergy,
friends, and donors was rich in insight.

In the summer of 1988, she responded to my frustra-
tions with my government work by reminding me that it is
"good to purify the 'politics' and make them for the glory of
God and the good of the people. If the politicians kept this
in mind—peace and joy will be in every human heart." Her
words were a spiritual booster shot, and I still cherish this
letter (at three pages the longest she ever wrote me), which
is full of spiritual guidance as well as the quotidian details of
running the ever-expanding MCs:

> Learn to pray the work. Do it with Jesus, for Jesus,
> to Jesus and in the midst of all gov work do it all for
> Jesus through Mary. You must bring holiness right
> there in the heart of government. I hope I will be
> able to meet the Yugoslav Amb. I don't know why
> this trouble—we now have four houses. I pray for
> you—for I am sure Jesus wants something more
> from you—to be His love, His presence right there
> where He has put you. Do not be afraid to accept an
> even higher position on condition that you be His
> love, His presence—that they look up and see only
> Jesus in you. The greatest love you can show me is
> that you love Jesus with all the tenderness of your
> love and keep your heart pure.

Father Brian Kolodiejchuk's anthology *Come Be My Light* reproduces many beautiful letters from Mother.

She was highly intelligent and intellectually curious. She spoke five languages fluently—Albanian, Serbo-Croatian, Bengali, Hindi, and English. And she was a powerful orator. Any audience could see plainly that she was the real deal. What's strange is how much she dreaded public speaking. She was fifty years old before she gave her first speech. In October 1960, she gave the keynote address at a gathering of the National Council of Catholic Women, in Las Vegas of all places. It was the first time she had left India in more than thirty years.

She never overcame her shyness and discomfort in the spotlight. She once told a friend that for her, facing the press "is more difficult than bathing a leper." But she came to accept the necessity of such duties. She felt God asked this of her and would give her the words to say, and it seems He always provided. As if to prove this, it was her practice to speak without notes. The only exception I remember was the speech at the National Prayer Breakfast in 1994. She was eighty-three and in poor health, and she wanted to be precise in her remarks about abortion as she addressed the nation's powerbrokers.

Mother was a champion of the right to life. She felt that to be pro-poor and pro-life were one and the same. For decades, she placed children unwanted by their parents in adoptive homes, and her houses for orphans took in children with birth defects and other developmental disabilities who were harder to place with families. She also opened homes for unwed mothers in many cities, including one just nine miles from the Hilton ballroom where she spoke that day.

"Any country that accepts abortion is not teaching its people to love, but to use any violence to get what they want," she said to the hushed audience. "This is why the greatest destroyer of love and peace is abortion."

Mary and I were there when she delivered these remarks and watched as the staunchly pro-choice president Bill Clinton, just a few feet away from Mother, repeatedly took sips from an empty coffee cup to hide any reaction. Only she could have delivered such a public scolding without controversy because she had not a hint of malice. Every word she uttered was said with love. The breakfast was the first time she met the Clintons, and she had a private talk with them after her speech. When I asked her later how the meeting had gone, she said only "We must pray for Mrs. Clinton." Mother often conveyed more by what she chose not to say.

As serious as she often was, her trademark smile was never far away and helped in such situations. Her cheerfulness was remarkable given the difficult life she chose. It was central to her work and mission. Each MC sister takes a vow of poverty, chastity, obedience, and wholehearted and free service to the poorest of the poor. The founding documents Mother wrote stress that each MC is expected to live these vows cheerfully. I recall a talk she gave in San Francisco in 1989 to a group of young women who were on the eve of taking their first vows. Mother was shockingly blunt: "If you can't be cheerful with the poor, then leave now. Go home." She said the poor had enough problems without a "helper" dragging them further down. She imitated a nun with a big frown, head down, walking dejectedly. The women all laughed, but they understood her point.

Mother's strengths as a leader made her admirable, but her weaknesses made her downright adorable. Everyone knew she had a sweet tooth. Once, when looking at the notebook she kept while studying with the Medical Mission Sisters in 1948, I found handwritten recipes for brownies, chocolate ice cream, baking powder biscuits, and sugar cookies tucked in the back. During the early years of the MCs, she partook of such treats only on special occasions like Christmas, Easter, and certain feast days, strictly adhering to her vow of poverty and setting a good example for the others. It was only as she got older that she allowed herself these small pleasures more frequently. And her sisters indulged her whenever they could.

She loved all things chocolate—ice cream and candies in particular. After her death, her close friend Sunita Kumar discovered Cadbury chocolates tucked away in Mother's desk drawer. But she would never eat sweets alone. These were for secret sharing. Once, I was traveling with her on a small plane, and after finishing her prayers, she offered the five of us candy she had stowed in her bag. She would not eat a piece unless each of us did. On an evening van ride from Los Angeles, she doled cookies out to us and herself, two at a time—twice. There was another time at lunch when I watched her break a cookie apart, piece by piece, savoring each bite. If she knew a sister liked sweets, she would sneak her some. She once was observed playfully telling one sister, "Eat this ice cream. I'll stand guard to make sure nobody sees you."

She delighted in giving gifts. She once handed me seven medals blessed at Lourdes, saying "I really spoil you!" Throughout the years I knew her, Mother made a habit of giving away belongings that were precious to her, such as her private prayer book, the crucifix she wore around her neck, her rosary, and the religious icons she loved. Once, when I was dropping her off at the airport, Mother's rosary snagged on her seat belt and the crucifix fell off. When I started to leave, she called me back: "Here, this is now yours," she said, putting it in my hand. She pointed out the tiny renderings of the Stations of the Cross that were etched on the back, which she said had often guided her meditations. It was an incredible keepsake. After I left, she turned to the friend she was traveling with and said, "That was a good thing I just did." She felt the glow and joy of giving. She delighted in letting go of such prized possessions. She knew the liberating influence of detachment and had frequently exhorted her sisters, "Let nothing and no one separate you from the love of Christ."

As astonishing as Mother Teresa was for all of us who knew her, she was not without faults. It doesn't serve her memory to pretend otherwise; her success in overcoming her faults makes her all the more admirable. A woman of action, she was famously impatient. "Meetings have a terrible sickening effect on me," she wrote to a priest. "It is a real sacrifice." "Sometimes I have been rather quick and harsh in voice when correcting the Sisters. Even with the people I have been impatient a few times," she admitted in another letter. Her impatience was paired with a formidable stubbornness. Those two traits are, perhaps, necessities for a saint's path of purification.

They may also have helped her to maintain a measure of detachment from her earthly suffering. In April 1942, she made a private vow to God "not to refuse him anything," and one of the things she gladly sacrificed for her work was her body. Her experience of "love until it hurts, give until it hurts" included a broken collarbone, a broken leg, a broken shoulder, and three fractured ribs in Rome, a compound fracture of her left arm (including protrusion of the bone) after falling out of bed, nineteen stitches in her head from a car accident in Darjeeling, and two stitches after being bitten by a dog in Delhi—followed by a series of painful injections to prevent rabies. Mother quietly suffered dozens of bouts of malaria, several rounds with pneumonia, tuberculosis, five heart attacks, a stroke, and two pacemaker surgeries. She had to be resuscitated on at least ten occasions after her heart stopped beating, and was put on a ventilator numerous times. She had deformed, misshapen feet from a lifetime of wearing donated sandals that weren't her size and disabling back pain that tormented her final months. She believed "suffering can become a means to greater love, and greater generosity," and she freely chose a penitential life.

Her obstinance also enhanced her effectiveness in dealing with worldly matters. For instance, when I was in Tijuana, Mother came to inspect the nearly completed seminary complex under construction for the MC Fathers. The concrete slabs had been poured, the cinder-block walls erected, the windows installed, and the roof securely put in place. The only task left was painting. The architect and a couple of the construction company executives proudly took Mother and some of the fathers on a tour of the facility as I tagged along. It was evident from the start that she was not pleased with the work. "It is too dark in these rooms," she told the group. They apologized but pointed out that the design plans agreed to by all parties had been scrupulously followed and insisted that nothing further could be done. This answer was not acceptable to Mother: "The fathers will need more light in here and air. I am sure there must be something you can do." They returned to the drawing board and came back with a solution that satisfied her: The crew lifted the roof off with a huge crane, added a series of windows and screens along the tops of all the walls, and then lowered the roof again and sealed it. When the seminary was opened in late 1989 and the men moved in, they were thankful for Mother's persistence.

Such stubbornness once drew a humorous rebuke from John Cardinal O'Connor, archbishop of New York. He was her dear friend, and someone she trusted. In May 1997, Mother was preparing to embark upon what she expected to be her final trip to the United States. Dr. Patricia Aubanel, one of her cardiologists, asked Cardinal O'Connor to try to convince her the trip was too dangerous. He called Mother in Rome, the first stop on her trip, and urged her not to continue on to America. Mother politely took his counsel and promptly ignored it.

She was in terrible shape when she arrived at the MCs' convent in the Bronx. Her back pain was so disabling she was confined to bed. But Cardinal O'Connor was celebrating Mass in the convent chapel the following morning, and Mother insisted on attending. She had to be wheeled in, and her friend began his homily by discussing her individual vows as a nun. "Mother Teresa, vow of poverty? Perfect. Mother Teresa, vow of chastity? Perfect. Mother Teresa, vow of charity? Perfect. Mother Teresa, vow of obedience? Never heard of it." The sisters in the chapel howled with delight. Mother herself laughed so hard that she rocked in her wheelchair.

Mother was a famously uncooperative patient. Dr. Aubanel told me, only half-joking, "She was the worst patient I ever had. I could not even tell her anything." And Mother only became less cooperative with age. When she was in the hospital in 1989, five days after her second heart attack, a doctor asked her what she was eating. With a twinkle in her eye, she answered, "An apple. An apple a day keeps the doctor away."

When she made up her mind to leave a hospital, there was no stopping her. She once walked out of a hospital in Rome with three fractured ribs from a fall, so determined was she to attend a ceremony of new sisters taking their vows. In 1996, the year before she died, she arrived back at the Calcutta motherhouse after a stay in intensive care and adamantly refused her sisters' pleas to carry her up the stairs in her wheelchair. Instead, she stood up and slowly walked up the twenty-six steep stairs, holding the rail as she went. When she reached the landing, she turned around to the sisters nervously gathered below and raised her fist triumphantly.

Dr. Lawrence Kline, a San Diego pulmonologist who met Mother in December 1990 when she was hospitalized at the Scripps Clinic with pneumonia, once tried to get Mother Teresa to have her lungs tested with the latest equipment. When she declined, he pressed: "Don't you think that God brought you here and that God would be happy to see you take this test?" "Don't bring God into this," she responded.

Mother could joke her way out of almost anything, particularly when she no longer was in charge. Sister Nirmala, a Hindu convert from a wealthy Nepali family and the seventy-fifth woman to join Mother, was elected her successor in March 1997. Within months, Mother was on bedrest with heart trouble and had two sisters supervising her care, Sister Shanti (a doctor) and Sister Luke (the nurse who ran Kalighat). They pleaded with Mother to stay at the motherhouse. But she wanted to greet Sister Nirmala at the Calcutta airport as she returned from her inaugural trip as MC superior general, and Mother convinced another sister to sneak her out in a car. Sister Luke and Sister Shanti tailed them in another car, bringing medical equipment and supplies in case of an emergency. When Mother saw Sister Luke and Sister Shanti at the airport, she smiled and mischievously said, "Well, hello! So good to see you here!"

I never once heard Mother speak derogatorily of or to anyone. But that did not mean she didn't get mad once in a while or wouldn't sharply correct you. The better she knew a person, the more direct the admonition. I was sitting near Mother during a Mass in Mexico attended by thousands, and when the priest invited the faithful to offer the sign of peace, a small stampede of children headed our way. When I tried to block them, Mother ordered me to "Let them come!" and shot me a look that should have turned me into a pillar of salt.

She occasionally raised her voice, and a number of her sisters have stories to tell. Sister Nirmala Maria, a trained nurse of Irish descent who, like Mother, began religious life with the Loreto sisters, knew how fragile Mother's back was, and once saw her bending over to fasten her sandals. She implored Mother, "Please don't do that. It is bad for your back." Mother shot back, "Don't talk to Mother that way!" On another occasion, the sisters in the Bronx wanted Mother, then well into her eighties, to get extra sleep. So they set the clocks ahead an hour so that Mother, a stickler for keeping to the community schedule, would think she was going to bed on time. After she lay down, the sisters secretly reconvened in another room, in the dark, to plan the next day's schedule. Mother caught them: "What are you doing up? You are supposed to be in bed!" One sister was so frightened by Mother's scolding that she actually ran from the room.

Inevitably, Mother also had disagreements with those closest to her. She once found herself at loggerheads with Brother Andrew, her handpicked head of the MC Brothers. "We are so different," Mother Teresa commented at the time, "but both of us have the same mind." They weren't always like-minded, however. He resisted her requests to have the brothers replicate identically the lifestyle of poverty her sisters embraced. She wanted uniformity, and he wanted the brothers to be more independent. For example, on occasion he allowed his men to sleep on the roof to escape their sweltering dormitories. Mother didn't allow this "luxury" for her sisters and objected. They scheduled a meeting to discuss the issue before the brothers' Holy Thursday service, which she was set to attend. Brother Andrew would not budge: "The Brothers have to decide this for ourselves or I go back to the Jesuits." She did not like his ultimatum and promptly left, attending the sacred liturgy at the motherhouse instead.

Three days later, on Easter, Mother returned to the brothers' house and told Brother Andrew that the men could decide such matters for themselves. "That was very grand of Mother," Brother Andrew later observed. They established a dynamic of mutual respect: "She gave me total freedom, even when she disagreed with me. But it has to be said that she could be annoyed and piqued—and show it."

If she could get angry, she was always quick to apologize or forgive. Mercy was her greatest trait—and her principal response to the call of Christ. "Be kind to each other," she exhorted her sisters. "I prefer you make mistakes in kindness— than that you work miracles in unkindness." This gentleness of spirit flowed from her merciful heart.

Pope Francis, although he met her only once, in 1994, recognized this. For the 2015–16 liturgical calendar, he instituted among the Catholic faithful a worldwide "Year of Mercy," which concluded triumphantly with her canonization. On that occasion he called her a "tireless worker of mercy," and remarked, "For Mother Teresa, mercy was the 'salt' that flavored her work."

He wasn't alone in drawing this conclusion. In the years after Mother Teresa's death, MC business and mission trips with students brought me to Calcutta sixteen times. On every trip, I sought out the surviving sisters from the original group who pioneered the Missionaries of Charity. These women seemed like veterans from a long-ago war, survivors of great spiritual combat. I wanted to know what it had been like to live in close quarters with Mother Teresa during those extraordinary years in the late 1940s and early '50s. Each of the nine sisters I spoke with mentioned, with fondness and admiration, her ability to forgive. Sister Monica, who entered in 1952, told me "her forgiveness" was Mother's greatest quality: "Mother always forgave so generously." Sister Margaret Mary, the eleventh woman to join, recounted how she once made an error in judgment in accepting a gift that went against their vow of poverty. Mother held her shoulders as she corrected her, but as soon as she finished, it was never mentioned again.

Sisters who knew Mother later echoed these sentiments. Sister Nirmala admired her ability to forgive: "She always would give one more chance to those who wanted it, as long as there was hope." Sister Mangala, an MC who knew Mother for more than twenty-five years, told me: "My favorite thing about Mother was how she would forgive and forget." Sister Prema, who joined the MCs in 1980 and would replace Sister Nirmala as their leader, recalled Mother saying, "If I judge you, I have no time to love you." "Mercy," she said, "had become second nature for Mother, and her whole attitude was putting herself into the shoes of other people, loving them and accepting them as they are."

Mother not only dispensed mercy—she sought it. She routinely asked forgiveness from God and whomever she offended. "Mother patiently and humbly stood in line for confession every week, as anybody else, to receive God's mercy," Sister Nirmala recalled. She sought absolution from others, too: In a private dispute with friends over a business matter in which I advised Mother, I saw a letter she had penned to the parties which asked for forgiveness for the way she had spoken and the hurt she had unintentionally caused. She went on to express her love for them and concluded with a second plea for forgiveness.

I once dared to correct Mother. She had written a letter

to President Clinton and asked an Indian businessman who was traveling to the United States to get it to the White House instead of sending it through the MC's usual channels. When I found out, I phoned her in Calcutta and shared my concerns about the haphazard transmission of such a highly sensitive communication. She didn't hesitate to apologize: "Ooh, I shouldn't have done that. I was wrong. I won't do that again." We both started laughing. It's hard to know which was more ridiculous: her repentance or my role as confessor.

| CHAPTER 9 |

A Joyful Christian

The miracle is not that we do this work, but that we are happy to do it.

—*Mother Teresa*

Mother Teresa thought that "joy is the net by which we catch souls." She knew that a fear-based, shame-based, or sin-based faith is joyless. Religion should not be a vehicle to vent anger, to judge others, and to nurture self-righteousness. Too many Christians, she knew, looked down scornfully at their fellow man, as if to say, "I'm right and you're wrong. I know the truth and you don't. I'm going to heaven and you're not."

No one can doubt the seriousness of Mother's beliefs. She knew full well that there was a happy ending to our earthly days and that God's promise of eternal life was reliable. But she was no dour Christian. Her smile was light itself. And she loved to laugh, most often at herself. Mother knew the importance of laughter in the midst of suffering. Unexpected moments of joy were reminders to her that God's faithfulness had the last word, not our own imperfection.

Saint Paul wrote, "Rejoice with those who rejoice, weep with those who weep. Have the same attitude toward all. Put away ambitious thoughts and associate with those who are lowly. Do not be wise in your own estimation." That was Mother. She did not let the devastating poverty and unrelenting misery in Calcutta—or anywhere else she opened a mission—deprive her of the joy of the Gospel. Her firm faith told her that suffering did not have the final word. And her beautiful human heart knew that she and her sisters needed to laugh and enjoy themselves as part of a balanced life. Without such moments of joy and release, the hardships they faced likely would have overwhelmed them.

She was full of quips that amused her friends and lightened the load of her sisters. When a friend told Mother she couldn't pick her up because she had a fever, Mother responded, "I also had a fever, but it is better to burn in this world than in the next." At a border checkpoint crossing into Gaza, she was asked by the guards if she was carrying any weapons. She replied, "Oh yes—my prayer books." One of her earlier followers, Sister Camillus, told me the story of how Mother reacted when she saw a young lady in a miniskirt. When the woman had passed out of earshot, Mother told a sister to go and get her a proper dress because she must be so poor she couldn't afford fabric.

Mother had a gift for knowing when to be serious and when to lighten things up. I think her sense of humor matured along with her relationship with Jesus. He, too, could appreciate a well-timed joke—he did, after all, make Peter pay his temple tax with a coin from the mouth of a fish.

Likewise, Mother's sense of humor and humility protected her, allowing her to remain a bystander to her own fame. When Malcolm Muggeridge's book *Something Beautiful for God* was published in 1971, he and Mother did a series of television and press interviews together. In the car between events, Muggeridge was paging through the *New York Times* when she saw an advertisement for the book featuring a large photo of herself. She wryly remarked, "There she is."

She was amused by her reputation for saintliness. Sandy McMurtrie was once riding in a car with Mother Teresa and Sister Priscilla, one of her trusted advisors, when the discussion began to annoy Sister Priscilla. Mother tapped Sandy and said, "To live with the saints in heaven is peace and glory; to live with a saint on earth is another story." Mother laughed heartily at her own joke. Sister Priscilla did not think it was funny.

Once we were crossing the border into the United States, in route from Tijuana to Brown Field Airport in San Diego, where Mother was scheduled to fly out on a small plane. After seeing Mother through the window and glancing at her Indian diplomatic passport, the immigration officer put a red card under my windshield wiper and ordered our van to "secondary inspection." This restricted area was where suspicious people were sent to be temporarily detained while their vehicles were inspected for illegal goods. I was dumbfounded. Did she think Mother Teresa was smuggling contraband into America? A friend, who frequently traveled with Mother, quipped, "The Soviets treat Mother better than the Americans."

I was growing angrier by the minute as drug-enforcement agents began to inspect our van. Mortified that my own country was treating Mother like a suspected criminal, I stormed over to the supervisor's office and loudly informed the official in charge that his people had just sent Mother Teresa of Calcutta to secondary inspection. He paled, jumped up from his desk, and rushed out to the area where she had been detained. By this time, Mother was outside the van, passing out sacred medals to the crowd of Americans and Mexicans who had surrounded her. The supervisor apologized profusely and sent us on our way. Through it all, Mother seemed amused, not offended, by the incident. She simply shrugged and said, "God must have wanted me to meet someone there."

With Mother, there was a time to be serious and a time to laugh. In 1989, she went to Phoenix for a prayer gathering of fifteen thousand people, which was attended by the governor of Arizona, Rose Mofford. I was supposed to pick Mother up when she returned to Tijuana the next day, so I telephoned the convent that evening to get her flight information. To my surprise, Mother answered the phone. When I asked her how the event went, she said, "We just got back. There were so many people there for one hour of prayer. I asked the lady from the government, in front of all those people, to give me a house. I told her that if she didn't, I'd bring the poor to her house." Then she added with impish delight, "Mother shouldn't have done that."

Mother often used jokes to gently nudge people into doing what she wanted. Sister Nirmala remembered such a time. She led the first MC expedition outside of India, a mission to Venezuela in 1965. "In Venezuela, it was very expensive to get drivers," she recalled. "Mother wrote to me, 'I want you to learn driving.' I was terrified. I thought I would not be able to control the car. It would run this side and that side and cause an accident. Just a few days before, and for the first time, I had sat behind the steering wheel with our parish priest. Big car, and with our priest beside me, I drove the car off the road. I scratched it against a building."

Frightened by this experience, Sister Nirmala wrote to Mother pleading to be excused from learning to drive. "Mother answered immediately. 'Sister,' she wrote from Calcutta, 'Our Lady drove a donkey to carry Jesus. I want you to drive a car to carry Jesus to the poorest of the poor.' That was enough. I learned how to drive," Nirmala said as she laughed at the memory. She also told me of a time when she drove Mother Teresa to a picnic on the Caribbean shore, and the joyful afternoon the sisters shared. "There, Mother relaxed with us and we played a board game, Ludo. And she laughed and laughed."

Mother Teresa could be downright playful at times with her sisters. During the feast day celebration of one of the nuns, the chocolate ice cream was so deeply frozen that it couldn't be scooped. Mother, by then into her eighties, told one of the sisters to go and get her a hammer. To the delight of her sisters, Mother hammered away at the ice cream right there on the community dining table in Calcutta, chipping off portions for the sisters to eat.

Sister Marelda, an MC sister I met in Calcutta in 2017, told me a story from years before: One day, she was cleaning the office in the motherhouse while Mother was working, when a large crate arrived. Inside the container was a statue of Mother Teresa's likeness seated in a posture of meditative prayer. Mother pulled the statue out, slapped it several times, and said, "Wake up! Wake up! Why are you sleeping?" Then she put the statue back in the crate and had it stored underneath a staircase where it remained until after her death. (The statue was eventually displayed in the chapel, in the spot where Mother used to sit.)

She could be quite mischievous with her sisters. When she was hospitalized in California in 1991, admirers sent her an array of get-well gifts. With her pulmonologist Dr. Kline and some of her sisters in her room, she opened a box to find a frilly nightgown. She held the lingerie up with a pencil, saying, "Look how nice it is!" The sisters and the doctor laughed out loud. When she found two pairs of matching underwear in the box, she exclaimed, "Oh, there is more!" Shrieks of laughter could be heard down the hallway.

I even witnessed her playfulness become unintentionally metaphorical. We were outside Tijuana looking at a potential site for a new seminary for the MC Fathers and had gathered for a prayer on the property. Father Joseph was praying out loud, when a baby rattlesnake slithered up behind Mother. I didn't want to interrupt the prayer, so I decided not to say anything unless the rattlesnake moved closer. As soon as Father Joseph was finished, I said firmly, "Mother, please don't turn around. Walk forward. There is a rattlesnake directly behind you." Instead, she turned around, saw the rattlesnake, and then bent over and shook her finger at it. "Oh, look at those eyes! So big! Wooo!" Would that Eve had done the same!

Her no-nonsense, take-charge management of situations great and small was interwoven with her complete trust in God. She often prayed in thanksgiving in advance for something she was about to request from divine providence. Sometimes, if her prayer wasn't answered promptly, she would stop herself and say to her sisters, "Well, we don't want to go faster than Jesus." And if her petition wasn't granted, she would remark, "If Jesus doesn't want it, then we don't want it."

When problems were truly intractable, she knew how to use humor to ease the anxiety. Mother Teresa spent six weeks in Amman, Jordan, in late summer 1970 to help establish a new mission for disabled children. Almost immediately after she departed, the Black September battles broke out between the Jordanian army and the PLO. The sisters mistook the sounds of bombs and gunfire for fireworks, assuming there must be a local celebration like the Hindi Diwali festival of lights. Within a week, the fighting edged close enough to their small convent that explosions shook the walls. A house on a nearby hill was bombed and completely destroyed.

One day a group of armed men searched their convent, looking for enemies or munitions. They left soon after, but the women were shaken. The fighting inched closer, and windows in the outer walls of their compound were shattered by the blast of heavy artillery. The sisters and the small group of children sheltering with them huddled in the inner hallways. At night, helicopters flew over the neighborhood searching for combatants. It was a harrowing time for the sisters and their neighbors.

When the nuns finally managed to get to a telephone,

they called Mother Teresa. "They told me about the violence, and they wanted to know if they should stay. I listened to them and we talked it over," she later recounted. "They were willing to stay there," and so she said to them, "Call me up when you are dead." It was the sort of moment of levity only she could carry off. The sisters laughed. Just hearing their mother's voice was all the assurance they needed, and the joke helped them cope. The sisters went back to praying, and soon thereafter, when the fighting ceased, they were instrumental in bringing food and medicine to the ill and wounded.

Jesus was playful with his followers, even in times of trouble. Three days after the Crucifixion, he approached two distressed followers on the road to Emmaus who did not recognize him, and asked what they were discussing. They could hardly believe anyone had not heard what had transpired in Jerusalem, and Jesus innocently asked, "What things?" as if he had been somewhere else. Jesus's gentle touch in responding to the anxiety or discouragement of those closest to him was a model for Mother Teresa as she led her sisters through their own trials.

Her readiness to laugh increased with age. She seemed to realize that as you get older, it is important not to take yourself too seriously. This principle was tested in the last year of her life thanks to an unflattering international media story: the "NunBun" fiasco.

I first learned of the story in January 1997 when the MCs in Calcutta faxed me the front page of a local newspaper that featured a story titled, "Is the NunBun a miracle?" An employee at the Bongo Java coffeehouse in Nashville, Tennessee, had unintentionally baked a cinnamon bun that bore "a striking resemblance" to Mother Teresa. The store owner, Bob Bernstein, capitalized on the opportunity for publicity, and Bongo Java started selling "Miraculous NunBun" T-shirts, "Bun Addiction" bookmarks, and prayer cards with the moniker "The Immaculate Confection." They also had a "Mother Teresa Special Blend Coffee" and coffee mugs bearing an image of the NunBun. The original had been shellacked for preservation, placed in a special glass case, and sent on a tour of area coffee shops. Jay Leno joked about the NunBun on *The Tonight Show*, and David Letterman did the same on *Late Night*.

All of this was in good fun, but as a lawyer, it also represented a breach of my client's privacy. I didn't believe Bongo Java had the right to appropriate Mother Teresa's image for commercial purposes, and judging from the media attention the NunBun was attracting, it was clear the owners were intent on cashing in. I wrote a cease and desist letter to which the response was an offer to make a charitable donation to the MCs. After I reported back to Calcutta that Bernstein was not going to stop selling NunBun merchandise, Mother Teresa wrote to him herself. She began, "I am writing to you to ask you to stop selling merchandise bearing my likeness. I have always refused permission for the use of my likeness for commercial ventures." After explaining to him that she would not accept any portion of the store's sales of Nun-Bun merchandise as he proposed, she concluded, "My legal counsel, Mr. Jim Towey, has written asking you to stop, and now I am personally asking you to stop. I do know that you have not done anything out of ill-will, and so trust that you will understand and respect my wish."

Mother's letter had barely arrived in Bernstein's hands before it was leaked to the local Nashville newspaper and reproduced in full: "Stop Selling 'NunBun,' Mother Teresa asks." The Associated Press had a story headlined "Mother Teresa Finds 'NunBun' in Poor Taste." The *Washington Post*'s take was similar: "Mother Teresa Nixes NunBun Profit." *Time* carried a "Mother Teresa Gets Tough" story that ended with the cryptic threat, "Mother Teresa's attorney Jim Towey intends to do something about it."

In the end, however, I didn't. Legal action would have only brought more attention to the story and increased Bongo Java's revenues. I thought it best to strike a deal allowing the shop to sell some items at the counter, as long as they did not use Mother's name or market the "Immaculate Confection"—and no more advertising on the Internet.

I had to present this compromise to Mother during her visit to New York in June 1997, but I dreaded bringing the subject up. How was I to remind her that people thought a cinnamon bun looked like her? I knew Mother wasn't vain in the slightest, but what woman wants to hear that the world thinks she looks like a pastry?

After starting our meeting with a number of pending business and legal matters, I turned to the matter of the NunBun. "Mother, I hate to bring this up, but I've spent the last five months trying to resolve a dispute about the unlawful use of your image." She was seated in her wheelchair, and Sister Nirmala, her newly elected successor, was standing to her right, slightly amused as she recognized the topic under discussion.

"Mother, remember the coffee shop in the U.S. that you wrote a letter to asking them to stop selling T-shirts of the

'Miraculous NunBun,' which had an image of a cinnamon bun that they felt looked like you?" I cringed as I said those last words.

Mother Teresa was nodding in recognition when a smile crawled across her face. Then she interrupted me and said, "Sister Nirmala is now the superior general. Ask them to put her face on the T-shirt."

Mother died before the settlement was finalized, so in the end the suit didn't matter. Without Mother, the NunBun schtick was no longer funny or interesting. God had stepped in and settled the matter.

| CHAPTER 10 |

In the Palace

Never seek the esteem of the worldly.

—*Mother Teresa*

At her address to the United Nations in 1985, Mother Teresa told the room full of dignitaries: "If Jesus puts you in the palace, be all for Jesus in the palace." It is a remark that has guided my life, and Mother practiced what she preached. Mother preferred the slums of Calcutta, but she often served as God's emissary to the palace—sometimes literally having to go to a palace.

Mother suffered considerably from this part of her calling, and even more so once she was a global celebrity. She was tiny and, during the years I knew her, increasingly frail. She disliked being hugged by strangers and often asked me to tell the people surrounding her not to tug on her or kiss her. The crowds that gathered around her everywhere felt suffocating. She described a 1976 visit to Philadelphia, with its swarms of people pressing upon her, as days "full of sacrifice. . . . I began to understand the Stations of the Cross with a deeper meaning. The police, the crowds, it all seemed as if Calvary [was] today being re-enacted all over again." She recognized the good that it did for the MCs and the poor, however. "This celebrity has been forced on me," she once said. "I use it for the love of Jesus. The press makes people aware of the poor, and that is worth any sacrifice on my part."

During the twelve years I knew Mother, her missionary travels rivaled those of Paul of Tarsus in apostolic times. Her home base was Calcutta, but unless she was hospitalized or recovering, she seldom stayed in one place for long. Every December and May, she routinely attended the ceremonies where her sisters took vows, and this meant travel to Rome, Washington, San Francisco, and elsewhere. Between 1985 and her death in 1997, the number of MCs increased in size by two-thirds, to nearly four thousand, which allowed her to staff over three hundred additional missions. The great majority of these new foundations were outside India, and by 1997, her missionary network extended to 120 countries. Mother attended the opening of these homes whenever she could, and as her health flagged, the sisters timed them to keep her away from the motherhouse during the hottest months in Calcutta.

The Vatican asked much of her as well. She and Pope John Paul II enjoyed an especially close relationship, which was a joy to both future saints. She was ten years his senior but always his loyal follower, and he never hesitated to make use of her charisma and charm in the service of the Church. Whether to the Synod of Bishops, the Eucharistic Congress, World Youth Day, or celebrations inaugurating years dedicated to Mary or the new evangelization, Mother

Teresa went wherever he asked. She opened homes in Cuba, Russia, Beirut, Romania, and other places where John Paul could not yet go—often laying the groundwork for the eventual papal visit. She was his loyal soldier, someone he could unfailingly count on, a faithful voice echoing the Catholic orthodoxy he espoused. "She had embodied many of what he regarded as the central themes of his pontificate—the defense of life, the defense of the family, concern for the poor, the dignity of women, the human rights of the humblest of men and women," wrote George Weigel, the preeminent biographer of the Polish pope.

She never said no to him, and her yes to John Paul went beyond mere obedience, to something more deeply personal, even maternal. When he was shot by a would-be assassin in May 1981, Mother Teresa immediately flew from Calcutta to Rome to visit him in the hospital. A year later when he returned from Portugal after another attempt on his life, she was there the next morning to see him.

There was real affection between the two. At a private audience when she brought her cardiologist for a courtesy visit to the pope, he greeted her with "Mother, my mother!" and bowed and kissed her hand. After accompanying her for a private audience, Mother's friend Sunita Kumar commented, "He treated her like *she* was the pope!"

Her influence on him was evident. "The Pope visited India to lift up the work of a great friend whose living embodiment of the Gospel of love he deemed the best method of advancing the Christian proposal in a culture deeply resistant to it," Weigel wrote. Soon after John Paul's return from that trip, which included a visit to Kalighat, he granted her long-standing request for a house within the walls of the Vatican to care for the hungry and homeless. Weigel described their relationship as "deep and intuitive," recalling the friendships of other saint contemporaries, such as Francis of Assisi and Clare, Francis de Sales and Jane de Chantal, and John of the Cross and Teresa of Avila. Mother and John Paul worked in tandem, using the media to help the poor and spread the Gospel, though he was far more comfortable under the klieg lights than she was.

Though the travel and public appearances on behalf of the Vatican and the MCs were hard on her, Mother rarely complained. She accepted the rigors of international travel and the glare of the media that her celebrity commanded.

Tennyson wrote, "We needs must love the highest when we see it." Mother personified this; everyone was simply drawn to her. In our troubled world, they were desperate to touch something better. Prominent people flocked to Mother. Former boxing heavyweight great Muhammad Ali was moved to tears after meeting her. Movie star Julia Roberts came to see her when Mother was recovering from an illness in California. Actress Penelope Cruz spent a week in Calcutta, assisting in an MC leprosy clinic, and reported after their meeting that she was "in awe of her."

Politicians around the globe sought her blessing just as she sought their aid in helping further her mission among their poorest citizens. Indira Gandhi, the leader of Mother's adopted country, was her friend for sixteen years. Shortly after Mother Teresa won the Nobel Peace Prize in 1979, Gandhi bestowed upon her the Bharat Ratna, India's highest civilian honor, and gave her a lifetime pass for free travel on Air India to help her spread her love and good works, saying "To meet her is to feel utterly humble, to sense the power of tenderness and the strength of love." The high regard seemed to be mutual. Mother praised the prime minister on one occasion for doing "a wonderful Christlike thing" in welcoming millions of refugees from Bangladesh. In 1984, Indira Gandhi was assassinated by members of her own security detail. At the funeral, Mother Teresa prayed that her Hindu friend's "soul live in peace forever."

American politicians of all stripes—from George H. W. Bush to Bill Clinton, Ted Kennedy to Pete Dominici—held her in high regard and asked to meet with her whenever she visited Washington. Bob Dole came to see Mother while he was running for president in 1996. They talked about her desire to get the MCs into China, and she gave him medals and her blessing. I once witnessed a private moment between Mother and Attorney General Janet Reno, during which she took Janet's hand and, finger by finger, counted out the five words that guided her life: "You did it to me."

No one met Mother and came away untouched. Ronald Reagan, Hillary Clinton, and Diana, Princess of Wales, could not have been more different as public figures. But in their encounters with Mother I observed a genuine connection and love. Each found in this tiny woman from Calcutta something rare for people caught in the klieg lights: a friend they could trust. Mother's love brightened their lives and was a balm to their souls.

Reagan had wasted no time in inviting her to the White House after his inauguration in 1981. The MCs enjoyed a long-standing partnership with the U.S. government, which had sent Mother aid through the United Nations and other nongovernmental organizations for decades. Mother Teresa told her friend Eileen Egan as they walked through Kalighat in 1957 that "foods from the American people have helped to bring these people back to life. America will be blessed for doing this thing." In 1979, she wrote to Jimmy Carter lauding America's generosity in providing food shipments to Catholic Relief Services: "Right from the beginning of the work—your people through Catholic Relief Services have shared the joy of feeding the hungry Christ clothing the naked Christ and giving a home to the homeless Christ. In all these years, nearly 30 years, your people have always been there. Thank God."

In Reagan, though, Mother found a friend and more. The president, like nearly everyone else, was awed by the diminutive nun six months his senior. Their first meeting took place barely two months after he had survived the assassination attempt by John Hinckley. Mother told him that all he had suffered had brought him closer to Jesus and the poor. So much for small talk! Asked by reporters later about his conversation with her, Reagan simply said, "I listened."

Her follow-up note included a warning to the president about the danger of nuclear war. "The presence of nuclear [arms] in the world has created fear and distrust among nations, as it is one more weapon to destroy human life—God's beautiful presence in the world. Just as abortion is used to kill the unborn child, this new weapon will become a means to eliminate the Poor of the World." Reagan surely respected her pure guilelessness. She was his kind of straight-shooter, and their friendship deepened over the years of his presidency.

When Mother Teresa was hospitalized in Rome in 1983 after her first heart attack, Reagan sent roses. He and First Lady Nancy Reagan met with Mother on numerous occasions, including twice in 1985. In June that year, the president bestowed upon her the highest civilian honor of the United States, the Presidential Medal of Freedom. After presenting the medal to her, he joked, "This is the first time I have given the Medal of Freedom with the intuition that the recipient might take it home, melt it down, sell the gold and spend the money on the poor." The president inscribed a photo of the event himself: "To Mother Teresa—with great appreciation and warmest affection. Sincerely, Nancy and Ronald Reagan." In the photo, he is clasping her hand with both of his, while Mother and the First Lady exchange loving smiles.

In Reagan's eyes, Mother Teresa could do no wrong. The White House staff sprang into action whenever sisters emigrating from India faced visa snags or she called to talk to the president. Brother Geoff, onetime leader of the MC Brothers, recalls Mother once using a public pay phone in India to place a call to the White House. She was put right through, and the two talked about famine relief for Ethiopia.

I didn't understand what a cherished friend he was for her until after he left office. In early 1989, she called and asked me to set up a meeting for her with the Reagans. When I reminded her that he was no longer in office, she said, "I know. That's why I want to see him now. I wonder if anyone goes to see him anymore."

Her solicitude for a friend who was no longer in power was touching. I scheduled the meeting for February 10, 1989, in Los Angeles. Covenant House, a nonprofit that helped runaways, sent a van to pick us up at the airport and drive us to Reagan's offices at Fox Plaza, where Secret Service personnel escorted us to a private elevator to the thirty-fourth floor. As Mother waited for her appointment, she asked me to refresh her memory: "What award did they give me? I think it was for peace?"

She met privately with both Reagans for about a half hour, and then her traveling companions were all brought in for a handshake and photo. By the time we returned to the lobby, word had circulated that Mother Teresa was in the building. Everyone from stockbrokers to snack-shop employees flocked to see her up close.

"That was very good that I visited him," Mother said when we were finally back in the van. She became almost chatty in talking about Reagan. "He was happy I came. At first, they were very formal. But then he relaxed. We talked about the Soviet Union. Mrs. Reagan said she would help when our MC Sisters come to Los Angeles. They were happy to see me. This time I came without anything to ask of him. I think that is good. Before I saw him as a president; today as a person." I had a sense she had found in the aging world leader something rare at that point in her life: a peer.

Hillary Clinton was first lady when she and Mother first met. They were on opposite sides when it came to the hot-button social issue of abortion. Mrs. Clinton was a forceful advocate for the legal right to abortion; Mother Teresa denounced it. Her opposition to abortion was a central component of every major public speech Mother ever delivered. In chapter eight, I described the anti-abortion remarks Mother made at the National Prayer Breakfast in Washington, D.C., in February 1994. It was after this speech that she met both Clintons. She and the first lady had agreed to work together to open a home for adoption in the Washington, D.C., area. She also intimated that the first lady had tears in her eyes by the end of their chat. "Mrs. Clinton has promised to give me a house for the children that nobody wants. I will write her a letter and then let us see."

She wrote two letters, the first addressed to both Clintons: "As per our conversation regarding saving unborn children from abortion through adoption I was very struck by your concern and readiness to help. . . . I pray that together we do something beautiful for God." Two days later in New York, she wrote a second letter to the first lady, reiterating her interest in opening the adoption home with her. She closed, "I often pray for you both. Keep the joy of loving in your hearts and share this joy with all you meet especially your family Kindly pray for our [MC] Society, our Poor, and for me."

Hillary Clinton was coming off a difficult year—she had taken a battering in the press over a major healthcare initiative—and seemed buoyed by this new friendship. In March 1995, she and her daughter, Chelsea, visited Mother Teresa's New Delhi home for children as part of their trip to India's capital. In a *Washington Post* opinion piece, Mrs. Clinton recalled their initial meeting: "It was February 1994, and she had just delivered a speech against abortion at the National Prayer Breakfast. . . . She told me about her homes for orphaned children in New Delhi and Calcutta and asked for my help in setting up a similar home. . . . Although we differ on some issues, we found common ground on adoption."

Sixteen months later, in June 1995, after much work,

the new adoption home opened on the western border of the District of Columbia. It was a large Tudor house in an upper-class residential neighborhood—not exactly in the mold of other MC houses throughout the world, but in keeping with Mother's practical directive that the home should be comfortable and welcoming to pregnant women and their babies. When Mrs. Clinton arrived at the home prior to the opening ceremony, I watched Mother walk over to her and greet her warmly. These unlikely partners had become fast friends. After the event, they worked the rope line together—the first lady guarded by her Secret Service detail, Mother by me.

When Mother Teresa died two years later, Mrs. Clinton led the U.S. delegation to the state funeral in Calcutta. Eunice Shriver, civil-rights icon John Lewis, and other political, religious, and business leaders were included in the group. Mary and I were both invited, but there was only one seat available on the official plane, so we had to choose who would go. Since Mary was still nursing our one-year-old son, we decided that I should go. Our delegation of fifteen would spend dozens of hours in transit, and be on the ground in Calcutta for just sixteen hours.

Several hours into the outbound segment of the flight, the first lady walked toward the back of the plane, where I was seated with Sister Dominga and Sister Therese-Marie, two MC representatives from the Bronx who were part of the delegation. I reintroduced myself and recalled how Mother frequently asked us to pray for the Clintons, and how pleased she was to have opened the adoption home with her. "Mother loved you," I told her.

The steely first lady melted like butter. "Mother used to send me handwritten notes from time to time, telling me what she was up to, that she was praying for me. I remember how badly she felt that she couldn't be with me in Delhi when I went there with Chelsea." She then paused, and added, "I get a lot of hate mail from Christians. I never understood why Mother loved me so much."

After the funeral and a brief visit to the MC orphanage, we stopped at the motherhouse so the first lady could offer her condolences to Sister Nirmala, and we said a prayer at the tomb, which local masons were still busy making. Then it was time to leave Calcutta. When I walked up the stairs onto the plane, Mrs. Clinton was standing at the door, giving a small aluminum medal to everyone as they boarded. "Sister Nirmala gave me these Miraculous Medals to give away," she explained. I had seen Mother Teresa place Miraculous Medals on land in Mexico where she wanted to build a seminary. Sister Marelda told me that Mother once put one on a sister's badly swollen hand, and it healed the next day. Mother had advised me to give them to people suffering from cancer, along with a special prayer and instructions on where to place the medal. But seeing Hillary Clinton distribute these amazed me, and I imagined Mother smiling at this scene from her new perch in heaven.

Mother Teresa's relationship with the Princess of Wales is the most surprising. They were an unlikely duo. One wore a cotton sari woven by lepers. The other was the embodiment of glamour in high-fashion clothes, designer pumps, and precious jewels. And yet, they had much in common. Both suffered from their fame—though the intensity of Diana's fame was far beyond what even Mother had to face. And they both were known for their compassion for the poor and particularly those suffering from AIDS. Both used their immense popularity to improve the plight of the downtrodden. They also shared a natural shyness and an aversion to photographers.

They are permanently linked in the public memory because Diana died just five days before Mother. The deaths of these two beloved women seemed to convulse the world in grief. Some Catholics feel Mother Teresa was slighted in the media as coverage of her death was overshadowed by the lead-up to Diana's funeral the following day. I do not see it that way. To me, God decided to let Mother Teresa slip out the back door in a manner befitting her simplicity and humility. The timing also gave India some measure of privacy to mourn the passing of its favorite adopted daughter.

When Diana went to Calcutta in February 1992 to meet Mother Teresa, she was already on the verge of separation from her husband. Mother was recovering from heart surgery and could not leave her bed to host the princess herself, but she ordered the MCs to roll out the red carpet for the occasion. A choir of hundreds of sisters welcomed their special guest. Diana wrote later that day to her friend and butler, Paul Burrell: "Today, something very profound touched my life—I went to Mother Teresa's home in Calcutta and found the direction I've been searching for all these years. The Sisters sang to me on arrival, a deeply spiritual experience and I soared to such great heights in my spirit."

This spiritual awakening led the princess to seek out Mother Teresa again a few weeks later, this time at the MC convent in Rome. The two visited for about a half hour and then prayed together privately in the convent chapel. The following year, Mother was in London and Diana was so eager to see her that she drove herself in her private car to the MC convent, not telling anyone in Kensington Palace and bringing along no security. The princess by this time was separated from her husband, and Sister Tanya, the superior of the London home, feels sure that she and Mother discussed the royal couple's situation. The princess had cried during their time together, and hugged Mother as she said goodbye.

In 1995, they were to meet again at the London convent, but when photographers swarmed the entrance, Mother changed the plans. "Better we go there," she told Sister Tanya. Arrangements were made for Mother to be driven through the side gate at Kensington Palace so she and the princess could have a private visit.

Sister Tanya, who was with Mother for each of these visits in London, felt the elderly nun's role with the princess was that of mother, confidante, and spiritual mentor. She says that Mother taught Princess Diana how to make the sign of the cross, discussed the Gospels, and prayed with her at the conclusion of each meeting. The princess needed someone to whom she could pour out her aching heart. But it was clear only God could help her. Mother became the mediator of this divine assistance.

After their meetings, Mother was tight-lipped with her sisters who inquired about what was discussed, only asking them to pray for the royal family. But, in 1996, she gave an interview to *Ladies' Home Journal* that caused all sorts of trouble. Mother rarely gave interviews. The journalist Daphne Barak had come to Calcutta seeking one and was sent off to Kalighat on Christmas Day to volunteer. She then got her face-to-face with Mother. In Barak's description, she "ended up holding hands with her, chatting like two teenage girls." Mother asked her if the stories that Princess Diana's marriage was over were true.

"It certainly appears to be," Barak replied.

Mother Teresa was quoted as responding, "I think it is a sad story. She is such a sad soul. She gives so much love, but she needs to get it back. You know what? It is good that it is over. Nobody was happy anyhow. . . . What will happen to the children? I hope they stay close to her. That is the only thing she has got."

These words caused quite a stir when they appeared in the article, as both the Catholic and mainstream press picked up on what appeared to be Mother Teresa's endorsement of divorce. Such a statement seemed contrary to everything she stood for, and more important to her, to the teachings of the Catholic Church.

I called Calcutta to report the media fallout and was asked to find out whether Barak's account was accurate. I spoke with Myrna Blyth, the editor in chief of *Ladies' Home Journal*, and she assured me the quote was 100 percent correct, though she refused to produce a recording of the interview. Mother didn't think she had said any such thing, but couldn't remember. She asked me to draft a statement, which she then edited and subsequently issued: "I do not know if this media account came about because of a misunderstanding, miscommunication, or mistake. I wish to make

A formal portrait of Mother Teresa from 1965, the year the Missionaries of Charity (MCs) opened their first mission outside of India.

Mother Teresa at Kalighat in 1980. It looked no different five years later when I had my first experience with the dying at bed 46.

A street kid sleeping on the pavement of an underground shopping center in Calcutta in 2019. The scene still haunts me; it is as if the boy fell out of the good life depicted in the mural above him.

Poor women queuing outside Mother's mission in Calcutta in 1980,

Mother with the Reagans in June 1985. She's holding the Presidential Medal of Freedom Ronald Reagan had just awarded her.

Mother riding in the popemobile with John Paul II in Calcutta on February 3, 1986. She called it "the greatest day of my life."

Senator Mark Hatfield and I enjoy a laugh with Mother in front of the MCs' Anacostia convent in June 1986.

President George H. W. Bush and First Lady Barbara Bush welcome Mother and Sister Dolores to the Oval Office in December 1991.

Princess Diana and Sister Frederick at the motherhouse in Calcutta in February 1992. Mother was sick that day but visited with Lady Di in Rome a few weeks later.

First Lady Hillary Clinton and her daughter, Chelsea, visiting an MC orphanage in Delhi in March 1995, accompanied by Sister Priscilla. Three months later, Hillary and Mother together opened the MCs' Washington home for adoption.

Mary (then Sister Katrina) and her Bronx superior, Sister Maria Lucy, welcome Harry and Ann Griffith, Mary's parents, for a visit in 1988.

On a congressional staff trip to Taiwan, Polly Gault and I visited the MC house in Taipei. I asked the sisters if I could have a photo with them, and Polly captured their surprise when I suddenly struck this pose.

Mother and I after an outdoor Mass in Tijuana, Mexico, in February 1989.

Mother handing out Miraculous Medals in Memphis, Tennessee, in June 1989. Sandy McMurtrie and I stood guard as hundreds filed past to receive one.

Mother connected with all mothers, here greeting a woman and her newborn in Tijuana in February 1989.

Mother sent thirty-five sisters to our wedding in Washington, D.C., in February 1992. Bishop William Curlin, Monsignor William Kerr, and Sandy McMurtrie joined us for the photo.

Sandy McMurtrie and Jan Petrie in 2016.

Roni Daniels, Mother's around-the-clock nurse in December 1996, with Sister Prema, the superior general of the MCs, in 2016.

MC Fathers Joseph Langford and Brian Kolodiejchuk in 1989.

The Kumar family (Jessima, Arjun, Gita, Preah, Naresh, and Sunita) with my son John in the Kumars' Calcutta home in May 2019.

I had just driven Mother to Gift of Peace in May 1986 and asked if I could take her photo to put in the MC prayer book she had given me. She not only agreed; she smiled.

Mother holding her lifeline, the rosary.

Dear Jim and Mary,
we send you this
with great love. You will
treasure this, for we
found it – in the drawer
of Mother table.
God bless you
M. Nirmala M.
15. 6. 2000

Mother's bedroom and office in the motherhouse in Calcutta.

This note from Sister Nirmala, and the family photo she included, came from Calcutta a couple of years after Mother died. She had kept it in her desk drawer, to our great surprise.

Mother holding Jamie when he was thirteen months old in February 1994.

Mother blessing a medal on Mary's chain a few hours after her National Prayer Breakfast speech in February 1994.

Jamie, two, giving Mother a blessing in June 1995. He had seen her do this with her sisters.

Mother greeting Joe, our second son, outside of Gift of Peace in June 1995.

Mother, in her wheelchair, accompanied by Sister Nirmala, giving out medals to our children ten weeks before she died, Bronx, June 1997. It was the last time I saw her.

Sister Francesca, a member of the original group of twelve that joined Mother in 1949, with Marie, John, and Mary in Saint Peter's Square in Rome for Mother's canonization Mass in September 2016.

Mother's body being carried from Saint Thomas Church to begin the procession to the state funeral. Hundreds of thousands lined the streets of Calcutta to catch one last glimpse of her.

Mother lying in state in Saint Thomas Church.

Mother's tomb in the motherhouse in Calcutta. Sisters often write message in marigolds on it.

The view from my seat in Saint Peter's Square moments before the canonization Mass began, September 2016.

Pope Francis celebrated the canonization Mass, and I did the first reading, September 2016. It remains one of the surest signs of God's kindness and mercy toward me.

The work goes on. Two sisters sign their final vows in the Gift of Peace chapel in Washington, D.C., in December 2020.

clear that I have never counseled anyone to seek a divorce." She referenced her "lifelong opposition to divorce" and added, "My love and fervent prayers are with the Royal Family during this difficult time." The *Washington Post* dubbed her clarification "Mother Teresa's royal retraction." Within five months the couple's divorce was finalized.

The last time Princess Diana and Mother Teresa met was in the Bronx on June 18, 1997, less than three months before their deaths. Diana had moved on with her life, focusing on her sons and her charitable activities. On that day, the princess met with First Lady Hillary Clinton in the morning at the White House, and then flew to New York to say goodbye to her "second mother," who was on what she planned as her final foreign trip. When their visit concluded, Mother walked hand in hand with the princess to the waiting motorcade. Diana stooped to kiss Mother's hands and head, and feel the warmth of the embrace of the woman who had changed the direction of her life. Shortly after the visit, Princess Diana donated seventy-nine of her dresses for auction at Christie's and directed that the $3.25 million in proceeds benefit AIDS and cancer patients.

Mother Teresa's last public statement in her life was one of condolence after her friend's tragic death: "She was very concerned for the poor. She was very anxious to do something for them. That is why she was close to me."

Both women had heartrending, globally televised send-offs. The "people's princess" had a royal funeral at Westminster Abbey, viewed by an estimated 2.5 billion people, with a performance by Elton John. For Mother's funeral, thirteen thousand invitation-only guests of diverse faiths, including myself and the other members of the U.S. delegation, filled an indoor arena in Calcutta. Before the Mass, a million Calcuttans lined the city's streets to see her body process by on the same gun carriage that had borne Mohandas Gandhi's in 1948. They had come to say goodbye to one of their own.

Before the princess was laid to rest in her tomb, the rosary beads a saint had given her were placed in her hands.

CHAPTER 11

Answering the Critics

Don't let his sin make you sin.

—*Mother Teresa*

It was a good thing that Mother Teresa had cultivated a capacity to forgive and bestow mercy because as her celebrity grew, so did the number—and vehemence—of her critics. Mother developed a thick skin. In all the years I represented her, she never defended herself publicly against the false claims or disparagement leveled at her. She felt God would protect her name if He had need of it.

The attacks took many forms. Some were simply criticisms of Catholic teaching (especially on abortion and contraception) in another form. A typical example was the feminist Germaine Greer criticizing Mother's anti-abortion views in response to the plight of rape victims in Bangladesh in the early 1970s who had become pregnant. "Mother Teresa offered them no option but to bear the offspring of hate. There is no room in Mother Teresa's universe for the moral priorities of others," she wrote.

The best known of Mother's critics was the journalist Christopher Hitchens, who made a habit of attacking her in columns, articles, and on television. Two years before her death, he published a book called *The Missionary Position*, which prosecuted a case against Mother Teresa along four principal lines. He accused her of cozying up to corrupt politicians and accepting ill-gotten gains from donors. He said that her homes provided substandard care. He claimed she both hoarded donations and misspent them. Finally, in criticism that can only be seen as *ad feminam* in nature, he called her a hypocrite, if not a fraud.

With the first line, Hitchens was essentially assailing Mother for the company she sometimes kept. He liked to draw attention to a photo of her with the then first lady of Haiti, Michele Duvalier, concluding that Mother was "licking the feet of the rich instead of washing the feet of the poor." Other critics also denounced her meeting with Fidel Castro, the dictator of Cuba. Duvalier and Castro were two in a long line of heads of state (and their spouses) who sought to meet with Mother and enjoy the inevitable favorable publicity. She agreed to these brief meetings as they were the price she had to pay for her sisters to reach the suffering poor in Haiti and Cuba. Mother was determined to get her nuns into the places with the greatest need. During their meeting, Castro told her that there were no poor people in Cuba, and Mother wisely responded that there must be elderly residents whom her sisters could visit. The gambit secured the permission she needed to open missions to help the island's downtrodden. To help Cubans is not to condone the Castro regime's crimes.

Mother opened MC houses in Eastern bloc countries well before the Berlin Wall came down in 1989, as well as in the Middle East and other areas of the world roiled by political and military strife. She engaged with politicians when necessary, but never their politics. Her high public profile made this an increasingly difficult tightrope to walk. Hitchens argued that Mother's dealing with the Duvaliers and Castros of the world made her "a political operative . . . an accomplice of worldly, secular powers." He simply misunderstood Mother's motives—or could conceive of no others. She knew that if Jesus could associate with prostitutes, eat with sinners, and peaceably interact with Roman oppressors, then she could be seen with corrupt leaders if that is what it took to serve the poor.

Mother understood authority and power. She never sought either, but she did seek to place these forces in the service of the powerless. Toward that end, she met with individuals of high wealth and influence throughout the world. These sought her out, and she made use of them.

One of Hitchens's favorite criticisms had to do with Mother's association with Charles Keating, a savings-and-loan tycoon and philanthropist from Arizona. He donated more than a million dollars to Mother for a new mission she opened in Phoenix. The Keating money was disbursed, years passed, and then he was indicted in California on charges of fraud, racketeering, and conspiracy. I briefed Mother on this development and how he was accused of wiping out the savings of many investors, including elderly ones. "Did he do this?" she asked. I told her he maintained his innocence but the evidence did not look good for him. She was saddened by this news and concerned for those who had lost their money. At no time during Mother's dealings with Keating did she have the slightest inkling that there were any concerns about his business ethics. Once she learned there were, she accepted no further Keating contributions and kept a proper distance from him so as not to bring scandal.

But she wasn't going to turn her back on him. After he was convicted, she wrote a letter to the sentencing judge asking for leniency. Hitchens had a field day with this. But then he would not recognize the precedent Jesus set. If He did not condemn a woman found under Mosaic law to be deserving of death, then Mother must have felt she could plead on her fallen friend's behalf. The co-prosecutor of the case made a very public request that Mother return the money. This was a bit of grandstanding since the Keating gift had been given under completely innocent circumstances years earlier, and the attorney didn't make this same appeal to the many other charities, churches, and politicians that had received Keating money over the years. Mother did not reply to his letter. She never discussed with me her reasons for not responding, but then she generally ignored her critics. And she knew the money had been given for the poor and had long since been used for their benefit. It was not hers to give back.

Guilt by association was a constant ploy for Hitchens and other critics of Mother. They often harped on the case of Donald J. McGuire, a priest well known to Mother and her sisters. I met McGuire in the late 1980s and was with Mother on several occasions when McGuire doled out the charm and piety to her in equal measures. He preached convincingly on Catholic teaching and spirituality and deftly infiltrated the MC's network of priest-helpers who conduct retreats, provide spiritual direction, and hear the confessions of the sisters. Nearly a decade after Mother's death, he was convicted in Wisconsin of sexually abusing two students, and in federal court two years later, of traveling to engage in sex acts with a teenage boy. He was sentenced to twenty-five years in a federal penitentiary. He remained stubbornly impenitent, never apologizing to his victims and dying behind bars in January 2017.

Mother was completely unaware of McGuire's dark side. She would never have associated with him, or allowed him around her sisters, if she had had any reason to believe he had betrayed his priesthood. McGuire avoided detection, ironically enough, by playing the victim card. He frequently represented to Mother that his Jesuit superiors investigated and persecuted him because his traditionalist views were at odds with theirs. He claimed they were intent on undermining his ministry. This was how he explained his temporary 1993 stay in a mental-health facility where the Jesuits had sent him for a psychological evaluation. Father John Hardon, another Jesuit, and a deservedly trusted associate of Mother, had been equally duped by McGuire. When she raised questions about McGuire's situation, Hardon always assured Mother of McGuire's innocence and uprightness, particularly during a visit to Calcutta in 1994, when McGuire was attempting to resume his ministry.

Shortly after that visit, a letter bearing Mother's signature and urging McGuire's prompt return to priestly service was sent to his Jesuit superior. This letter came to light during McGuire's trial in 2006 and was published as an exposé in

2012. Having seen it, I am certain it was not composed or prepared by Mother or any of her sisters. To start, the letter was dated in the American style, which states the month first; Mother dated her letters in the European style, starting with the day. It was typed on the wrong letterhead—even the paper size was wrong—and Mother, moreover, nearly always handwrote sensitive correspondence. The letter included phrases she never employed, referring to her regional superiors as "regional assistants," for instance, and four elected counselors as "my four assistants." Most telling, it includes a list of McGuire's retreats with the names of the thirteen sisters who had organized them, which could have only come from him, not Mother. The letter almost certainly was drafted by McGuire, or at his direction, and Mother simply signed it unread when it was handed to her by someone she trusted, most likely Father Hardon.

Media accounts at the time of McGuire's trial portrayed him as Mother Teresa's spiritual confidant, a misrepresentation that McGuire himself promoted. In a promotional flier he circulated the year Mother died, he described himself as "Mother Teresa's Retreat Master." Hundreds of priests over the years heard Mother Teresa's confession or oversaw retreats for her or her sisters. McGuire was not her spiritual director or regular confessor, though he schemed tirelessly to convince everyone he was.

Although Mother Teresa did nothing wrong and reasonably relied on Father Hardon's representations of McGuire, the shadow of her association with the disgraced former priest will linger. Had she lived to learn of McGuire's moral depravity, her concern would not have been for her reputation. Instead, she would have grieved for his victims, their families, and all those who had been scandalized by his gross, criminal misconduct. Her heart would have been broken over the damage he had done, just like any mother's.

Mother Teresa's approach to caring for the poor was a second focus of criticism. This was the go-to complaint of Aroup Chatterjee, a Calcutta-educated but London-based physician. He complained that her programs were too primitive. Kalighat, her home for the dying in Calcutta, was one of his and Hitchens's prime targets. "The care facilities are grotesquely simple: rudimentary, unscientific, miles behind any modern conception of what medical science is supposed to do," Hitchens opined. They demanded an upgrade in the level of care Mother offered, arguing that she had the resources to bring in modern medical equipment and trained professionals.

But the MCs were not running a hospital. The sisters were compelled by faith to help the waves of desperate people dying on the pavement outside their doors. They were responding to "Jesus in his distressing disguise." Kalighat was a home where the dying could be known by name, kept clean, treated as family, and most of all, loved and accompanied in their last days. The sisters never charged anyone a rupee for their services, which did include some emergency medical care. I saw on numerous occasions sisters patiently using tweezers to pick maggots out of large wounds in patients' skulls (where the brain was actually exposed) and in legs (where the bones were showing). They couldn't send their patients to the area hospitals because those institutions did not receive the destitute. Applying a first-world standard to the challenges the MCs faced operating a residential facility like Kalighat is ludicrous. Pain medicines, antibiotics, and many necessary supplies were routinely unavailable. They made do with what they had, and the dying were better off for their efforts, "rudimentary" or not.

Hitchens vacillated between claiming that Mother didn't care about her charges' suffering and arguing that she wanted them to suffer because of her religious views. It is hard to take such accusations seriously. I can think of no one in the twentieth century who did more to alleviate suffering than Mother Teresa. The MCs were not equipped to treat pain the way a modern hospital or hospice might, but they made the residents of Kalighat comfortable. Did the MCs sometimes use the same hypodermic needle or latex gloves with more than one resident? Yes, but this was because of supply lines that remained unreliable for many years. There was no choice but to sanitize and reuse what was on hand. No one died because of this practice. What's more, a visit to Kalighat today presents a different picture because the MCs and the city have improved their systems. Analgesics, IVs, and other medical interventions are now regularly available to the MCs thanks to huge advances in India and around the world.

Many critics wanted Mother Teresa to go beyond ameliorating the misery of the poor to addressing the societal problems that created poverty in the first place. She was quick to respond that this was not her mission. "We all have a duty to serve God where we feel called," she wrote. "I feel called to help individuals, not to interest myself in structures or institutions." Mother stressed that the sisters were neither social workers nor an extension of government. They were nuns living out their love of God through daily work. Critics were free to open and operate clinics or feeding centers according to their high ideals. There is a Spanish proverb that says, "It is not the same thing to talk of bulls as to be in the bullring." These critics assiduously avoided the bullring. Had they actually undertaken hands-on work with the poor, they would have seen the immense challenges Mother Teresa—and all those caring for the hungry, sick, and dying—faced.

As for how Mother Teresa managed money, Hitchens and Chatterjee were fond of portraying her as a hoarder, flush with cash, who forced her followers to embrace poverty and beg for handouts. "Under the cloak of avowed poverty they were still soliciting donations, labor, food, and so on from local merchants," despite having sizeable bank balances, wrote Hitchens.

It is important to note that the MCs don't solicit donations. Mother strictly prohibited fundraising. Money comes to the MCs because people make charitable contributions and estate gifts of their own free will. The Missionaries of Charity shepherded what they received for current or future needs. It is true that Mother was frugal. She and her sisters wasted nothing. They knew the difference a few dollars would make among the penniless and sought to honor such poverty through careful stewardship. The MCs' vow of poverty cultivated an ethic to waste nothing. I saw this play out when I ate lunch with Mother and watched her pick up and eat with her fingers every solitary grain of rice on her plate. Her sari was often threadbare, and she mended the rips in the fabric rather than replace the garment. Because Mother would not trade out her old saris for new ones, the sisters had a similarly tiny nun wear in a substitute for weeks before they surreptitiously switched it for Mother's.

When Hitchens wasn't criticizing Mother Teresa for her frugality, he was lambasting her for spending too much. "The vast sums of money she raised were spent mainly on building convents in her own honor," he claimed. Here, too, Hitchens was completely wrong. The MCs rarely built new convents. They were the beneficiaries of abandoned convents and other donated buildings in the places they served; only a small percentage of their funds ever went to the purchase or refurbishing of properties. And wherever she opened missions, there were generous individuals who sought Mother out, and she joined forces with them. Dwayne Andreas, the longtime CEO of the multinational agricultural company Archer Daniels Midland (and Sandy McMurtrie's father), teamed with her to send tons of food in containers to Haiti and other developing countries. Tom Flatley, a property developer in Boston, purchased two houses in Massachusetts for the MCs to shelter women and children. In 1989, Tom Owens, an IBM executive, helped Mother build a children's home in Tijuana. She sat down with him and, with a blue felt pen, drew on a white paper napkin a room-by-room design of the house she envisioned. Tom and I sat there in amazement as she detailed her vision. She designated one room for children with tuberculosis as the "TB room." Tom misheard her and promised to put in a large TV for the kids, which got a good laugh from Mother. He paid for the construction of that house according to the specs Mother sketched; it opened the next year and to this day shelters dozens of children. Mother did not see the world as comprised of the rich and poor and everyone in between. She did not judge those well-off, but she did make them feel that she could put their money to good use.

Mother's wisdom in not wasting money and building a small nest egg has been vindicated. Funds raised during her lifetime still subsidize the worldwide network of charitable programs she built. The account balances the missionaries maintain aren't nearly as large as in the late nineties, but the MCs are unconcerned. They depend on divine providence, and God continues to provide.

Hitchens's most scathing criticisms were directed at Mother Teresa personally. In his eyes, she was a hypocrite and deceiver who promoted a "myth of saintliness." To an atheist like Hitchens, it seemed she was projecting a lifestyle of the poor while enjoying the spoils of the elite. It is true that Mother Teresa flew first class on commercial airliners from time to time. (Germaine Greer once shared the same cabin with her and disapproved of how Mother neither ate, drank, nor left her seat during the flight.) Mother flew first class because the airlines begged her to; her presence in coach caused such a huge commotion that flight attendants could not attend to the other passengers. Mother thought nothing of the luxury and simply did what the airline thought best for all.

In the latter years of her life, she accepted offers from individuals she knew to fly on their private aircrafts. This convenience enabled her to spend more time in her missions and less time in airports. It had the added benefit of allowing her to get rest as she went from city to city. She did not pay a penny for such flights. She never sought the special treatment she received. Had it been up to her, she gladly would have remained in Calcutta and never traveled. But she felt it her duty to journey regularly to the missions she had fostered across the world and also serve as an ambassador for Pope John Paul II when he requested it.

Mother Teresa did not leave India once in the first thirty years she lived there and cannot be credibly accused of jet-setting. I traveled with her on private planes on several occasions. Her routine was always the same: board the aircraft, pray the rosary, talk business if necessary, eat whatever food was provided, stare out the window, and, if possible, drift off to sleep. She wasn't in the slightest way seduced by the amenities at her disposal, although she did enjoy cashews when they were offered. As her mission grew, she had learned to be "all for Jesus in the palace"—even if that meant in a flying one. She considered such niceties to be gifts from God. They stood in stark contrast to the thousands of comfortless trips she took in crowded trains, trams, vans, and beaten-up cars, which were her usual modes of transportation.

As for her own health, Hitchens relished pointing out the instances of her being admitted to first-rate hospitals during times of grave illness, contrasting that to the plight of the poor who are denied such privileges. Again, Hitchens misrepresented what actually took place. Mother accepted the generosity of hospitals and professionals who were happy to provide their services to her without charge. They knew of her selfless life and wanted to do something in return. But when it came to the choice of where she would be treated and by whom, she was a bystander to those decisions. She gladly accepted the charity. She felt that any money she didn't have to spend for medical services could be spent on the poor.

The irony of Hitchens's criticism here is that Mother Teresa didn't want to be in a hospital in the first place. When I visited her in a Calcutta intensive care unit in 1996, she pleaded with me to take her back to the motherhouse. From the early 1940s when she resisted rest even though she was at the brink of a breakdown, she maintained a lifelong aversion to hospitals, even when she was gravely ill. Hitchens and Chatterjee's suggestion that Mother Teresa relished preferential medical treatment had the appearance of truth, but could not have been more false.

Perhaps the most offensive of the criticisms leveled against Mother Teresa was that she used the poor to advance her personal agenda—that she was "less interested in helping the poor than using them as an indefatigable source of wretchedness on which to fuel the expansion of her fundamentalist Roman Catholic beliefs," as one reviewer summarized Hitchens's thoughts. How Hitchens could visit Kalighat and walk around Calcutta with her (as he did once in 1980) and conclude "she was not a friend of the poor; she was a friend of poverty" defies rational explanation. For decades, Mother Teresa had personally tended to the wounds of lepers, bathed the bodies of the dying, fed malnourished refugees, and sheltered orphans and the developmentally disabled in utter obscurity. Hitchens focused on Mother toward the end of her life when her responsibilities to administer a worldwide organization required her to travel outside India, and her poor health often prevented her from the daily direct contact with the needy that she had known and, quite frankly, preferred. Perhaps this skewed his evaluation. But it bears repeating that those quickest to criticize Mother were seldom inclined to do the work she did, even for a day.

One cannot research the criticisms of Mother Teresa without running into another well-worn charge, typically sourced to a former MC or Kalighat volunteer—that she took advantage of vulnerable, dying people and coerced them to convert to Christianity. Yet there is not a single eyewitness account of Mother Teresa ever baptizing anyone without their consent. The sketchy anecdotal evidence Hitchens and Chatterjee offer as proof belies her lifelong practice of not forcing her religion on those she served. If any sister secretly baptized residents without consent, they did so in violation of Mother's explicit orders.

This is not to say Mother Teresa was indifferent toward the eternal destinies of others. She was a Christian missionary and longed for people to come closer to the God she loved. But she respected the individual faiths of all the people she and the MCs served. "I love all religions, but I am in love with my own," she once said. "There is only one God and He is God to all; therefore it is important that everyone is seen as equal before God. I've always said we should help a Hindu become a better Hindu, a Muslim become a better Muslim, a Catholic become a better Catholic." She often stressed that she converted no one and that only God could. In Kalighat, where tens of thousands died and even more recovered, Mother Teresa prayed with the residents and commended them to God's merciful care. She helped them find peace in their own way as they left this world. She made no claim as to what God did with their souls after death; the mechanics of salvation were not her concern. She did not believe only Christians made it to heaven.

After Mother Teresa's death, the claims of her detractors became much more mean-spirited. Hitchens called her "a sly and worldly sinner" in *Vanity Fair* and declared that "my day of vindication may come, though it will be scant comfort to be joined in hell by an unsmiling nun." And they haven't abated a quarter of a century later. In 2021, Michelle Goldberg, a *New York Times* columnist, wrote a piece entitled "Was Mother Teresa a Cult Leader?" Goldberg's line of argument was nothing new and mostly echoed Hitchens's charge that Mother promoted a "cult of death and suffering." Or "fetishized suffering rather than sought to alleviate it," as Goldberg put it. Her hook was a ten-part podcast called *The Turning: The Sisters Who Left*, coproduced by Mary Johnson, an ex-sister who has long broadcast her dissatisfaction with the MCs. The series opens with her discussing her yearning to flee the order and how she felt she was kept from doing so. Her own memoir of her time in the MCs details her sexual desires and how these took her away from her vows. She certainly lied to Mother Teresa when confronted by a report that she had been discovered in bed with a woman under her supervision. Johnson's book includes all the ways she betrayed Mother Teresa's trust. Through it all, Mother treated Johnson as kindly as Jesus treated Judas.

Goldberg, though, took Johnson's story at face value and justified her own attack as part of "a broader drive in American culture to expose iniquitous power relations and re-evaluate revered historical figures." And, predictably enough, this "re-evaluation" indicts Mother Teresa and the thousands of women who continue her work, many risking their lives in places like Yemen, Syria, Iraq, and other countries torn by violence. For Goldberg, the testimonies of a handful of former MCs make a case that the sisters who stayed were brainwashed captives living in a "hive of psychological abuse and coercion."

Unanswered by Goldberg were two basic questions: First, if Johnson and these women were so miserable, why did they stay so long? They knew from day one they could quit the convent at any time. And second, if convent life is so awful, why do thousands of MC nuns, serving in the most impoverished and dangerous places on earth, stay? Goldberg ignored these obvious defects in her polemic. Instead, she concluded, "Viewed through a contemporary and secular lens, a community built around a charismatic founder and dedicated to the lionization of suffering and the annihilation of female selfhood doesn't seem blessed and ethereal. It seems sinister."

It's the Hitchens problem all over again. A "contemporary and secular lens" can never see the lives of Mother and her sisters as they are—generous, fulfilling, courageous, and joyful. Goldberg is mystified that a love for God could inspire someone to leave family, forgo children of their own, and renounce the comforts of the world to serve the poorest of God's people. The MCs never claim to be perfect, and neither did Mother. She was the first to point out her own weaknesses and failures. Perhaps that is why she needed God so much.

Mother Teresa once told me that she forgave Christopher Hitchens for his book, even if she didn't understand why he wrote what he did. And I am certain she would have forgiven Mary Johnson if her grievances had been publicized during her lifetime. Reluctantly I must conclude that if she could forgive her critics, then those who love her should do the same. But people like Hitchens, Chatterjee, and Goldberg don't make that task easy.

CHAPTER 12

In Darkness as in Light

I am learning to want what He gives and not what
I prefer.

—*Mother Teresa*

Jesus said, "Whoever wishes to be my follower must deny
his very self, take up his cross each day, and follow in my
steps." Mother Teresa picked up her cross at every opportunity: seeking, in her own words, "always the hardest." In the
Calcutta motherhouse, she took for herself the worst room
(the hot one above the coal-burning stoves in the kitchen),
the worst chores (cleaning latrines, scrubbing floors), and
the worst food (whatever was left over after others had been
served). The crucifix pinned to her sari, the crucifix on the
rosary that was constantly in her hand, and the large crucifix
she secured in the fold of her sari at the waist each morning,
served as constant reminders of what God asked of her.

The weight of her cross, though, included suffering that
she did not choose—trials that were imposed upon her by God.
For in addition to the many physical, mental, and emotional

burdens she carried as head of a missionary order, Mother endured nearly five decades of punishing spiritual pain. It nearly suffocated her soul. This was a private struggle, shared only with her confessors and with Archbishop Perier of Calcutta. That it came to light is due to the correspondence collected by Father Brian Kolodiejchuk as part of the Vatican's documentation-gathering process for determining sainthood. He found letters from the archdiocese of Calcutta archive that had been preserved from the 1940s and 1950s, as well as Mother's own journals from the time after she left Loreto. Mother never meant for these writings to survive. Father Neuner, an Austrian-born theologian who counseled her through some of her most painful moments, testified in the canonization process: "She gave me the papers with the explicit request to burn them as soon as I had read them." After much prayer and consultation, Father Brian reproduced more than 150 of Mother's letters and notes in the book *Come Be My Light* (2007). He believed her own words would contribute to a richer understanding of her life. The collection reveals her experience of darkness and her years of estrangement from God, a spiritual state Catholics know as the "dark night of the soul."

She first revealed this darkness, which persisted for nearly the remainder of her life, in a March 1953 letter she wrote to Archbishop Perier. "Please pray specially for me that I may not spoil His work and that Our Lord may show Himself— for there is such terrible darkness within me, as if everything was dead. It has been like this more or less from the time I started 'the work.' Ask Our Lord to give me courage." Except for a five-week period in 1958 when she received a brief

respite from "that strange suffering of ten years" after praying to the newly deceased Pope Pius XII and asking him for
a sign that God was pleased with her endeavors, the intense
suffering and estrangement from God she experienced never
subsided.

"Lord, my God, who am I that You should forsake me?"
she wrote in a 1959 letter to Father Lawrence Picachy, her
confessor at the time. "Where is my Faith?—Even deep
down, right in, there is nothing but emptiness and darkness.
My God—how painful is this unknown pain. It pains without ceasing.—I have no faith.—I dare not utter the words and
thoughts that crowd in my heart—and make me suffer untold
agony." She put these feelings on paper out of an inability to
talk aloud about them, even to her confessor, and to ease her
inner agony. "Thoughts put on paper give a short relief," she
wrote. "Why He wants me to tell you all these I don't know."

In 1959, Father Picachy requested that she address a letter directly to Jesus. "In my soul," Mother wrote, "I feel just
that terrible pain of loss—of God not wanting me—of God
not being God—of God not really existing (Jesus, please forgive my blasphemies—I have been told to write everything)."

The letters outline the agony of a woman completely
devoted to God who felt no love in return. "In the call You
said that I would have to suffer much," she wrote, recalling Jesus's message to her on the train to Darjeeling. She
worked herself to the bone trying to quench Jesus's thirst
for souls, and yet she wrote in another letter, "Souls hold no
attraction—Heaven means nothing—to me it looks like an
empty place."

When Father Brian sent me the galley proofs of *Come Be*

My Light to review before they were published, I was shocked by what I read. Mother felt God did not want her? Darkness surrounded her on all sides? It was impossible for me at first to reconcile what I read in her letters with the joyful woman I knew, a woman who seemed spoiled by God. Those who were close to her saw that she lived an incredibly difficult life in the most trying of environments, giving her all, refusing God nothing. We just assumed that in return, God was whispering sweet nothings into her ear and comforting her in the quiet of prayer. The book's expressions of inner pain and loneliness remain hard to reconcile with my memories, but I recognize the words as unmistakably hers.

Reading the book, it felt as though Mother were suddenly a stranger to me. I pored over the letters for clues that might reveal how it was possible for her to be in such pain and yet be so cheerful all the time. "People say they are drawn closer to God—seeing my strong faith.—Is this not deceiving people? Every time I have wanted to tell the truth—'that I have no faith'—the words just do not come—my mouth remains closed.—And yet I still keep on smiling at God and all," she wrote in 1962, twelve years into her journey of darkness. I was one of those people who saw strength in her faith; I was drawn closer to God by her beatific smile and what appeared to be her firm convictions about God. Had she told me that she had no faith, I wouldn't have believed her. And yet her letters describe a woman who spent the last fifty years of her life in spiritual darkness, deprived of any sense of God's presence or love for her. If Mother Teresa entertained doubts about the existence of God, what can those of us of lesser faith expect?

I immediately contacted friends from the MCs: Sister

Nirmala, Father Joseph, and other sisters and priests who knew Mother far better than I. Were they aware of what she had suffered all those years? They all had the same response: She had never mentioned a thing. This was as astounding to me as her painful concealed darkness itself. Had it been me, I would have found ways to let my intimates know the extent of my anguish. But Mother chose to bear these trials privately, to carry her cross alone.

The more I thought about what the letters revealed, the more I came to see Mother Teresa's darkness as a share in the agonies and passion of her Savior. As Saint Paul wrote of his own spiritual travails, "Even now I find my joy in the suffering I endure for you. In my own flesh I fill up what is lacking in the sufferings of Christ for the sake of his body, the church." The Gospel of Mark's account of the crucifixion begins, "When noon came, darkness fell on the whole countryside." And Jesus cries from the cross "in a loud voice, 'Eloi, Eloi, lama sabachthani?' which means, 'My God, my God, why have you forsaken me?'"

Mother Teresa mysteriously shared in His darkness and sense of abandonment. "In my heart there is no faith—no love—no trust—there is so much pain—the pain of longing, the pain of not being wanted," she wrote in 1959. "I don't pray any longer—I utter words of community prayers—and try my utmost to get out of every word the sweetness it has to give." She may have felt forsaken and forgotten by God, and struggled with doubts about God's existence during her most trying moments, but the darkness that shrouded her life until her death did not have the last word. To the end she clung to a blind trust in a loving God.

She ultimately reached a level of enlightenment about the role darkness played in her life and vocation. In a 1961 letter to Father Joseph Neuner, she wrote, "For the first time in this 11 years—I have come to love the darkness. For I believe now that it is a part, a very, very small part of Jesus' darkness and pain on earth. . . . More than ever I surrender myself to Him." She had learned to embrace the darkness that fell on her soul, befriend it, and offer it back to Jesus. Toward the end of her life, she confided in William Curlin, bishop of Charlotte, North Carolina, whom she had first met at the Gift of Peace when he was a parish priest. "What a wonderful gift from God," she wrote to Curlin, "to be able to offer Him the emptiness I feel. I am so happy to give Him this gift."

Mother's letters also suggest that the experience of rejection enabled her to identify more closely with the lepers and outcasts of Calcutta who well knew the pain of being unloved and unwanted. In 1962, she wrote, "The physical situation of my poor left in the streets unwanted, unloved, unclaimed—are the true picture of my own spiritual life." I have often pondered the coincidence of the onset of her spiritual trials just as the charitable work of the Missionaries of Charity began to flourish. It seems that the more Mother Teresa felt rejected by God, the more her mission of bringing the love of God and relief to the poor thrived. Was darkness the price she had to pay? If so, I know that she was happy to pay it.

"Instead of stifling her missionary impulse, the darkness seemed to invigorate it," Father Brian observed in *Come Be My Light*. "Mother Teresa understood the anguish of the human soul that felt the absence of God, and she yearned to light the light of Christ's love in the 'dark hole' of every heart buried in destitution, loneliness, or rejection. She recognized that whatever her interior state, God's tender care was always there, manifested through the small favors others did for her or unexpected conveniences that accompanied her undertakings." Indeed, the poor were her window to God when she felt the door was locked to her. As Father Brian wrote, "At prayer she would turn to Jesus and express her painful longing for Him. But it was only when she was with the poor that she perceived His presence vividly."

The extraordinary, supernatural encounters with Jesus that Mother had, and the prolonged dark night of the soul that followed, were meant to be her secret—a private matter between herself and God. She described her mystical calling as "a delicate gift of God to me" and explained to one sister that she never discussed the inspiration for the Missionaries of Charity because "when you make it public it loses its sanctity." Indeed, she wanted to keep her suffering to herself, but she told her confessor that God Himself insisted that she reveal her interior darkness. She wrote these letters for her confessors, but because the experiences she related to them were not sinful in nature, they fell outside the "priest-penitent" protections that would have kept such private communications permanently privileged.

Mother instinctively knew that words were incapable of communicating "the deep things of God," and that the mere fact of writing such things diminished them. The great medieval theologian Thomas Aquinas discovered this truth three months before his death when he received a direct revelation while celebrating Mass. "I have seen things that make my writings like straw," he declared, and he never wrote another word.

Mother also feared the writings would become a distraction if they were made public. "Please do not give anything of 1946," she begged Archbishop Perier in 1957. "I want the work to remain only His. When the beginning will be known people will think more of me—less of Jesus." She begged Father Picachy to "destroy everything that I have written to you." Mother's appeals went unheeded. The archbishop and her confessors maintained strict confidentiality during her lifetime, but they believed her writings belonged in the treasury of the Catholic Church for all to see.

While the letters sparked a great deal of interest and even controversy during her canonization process, in the end they simply allow for a greater understanding of her holiness. Her life was ultimately judged heroically virtuous by multiple criteria: her work with the poor, the testimony of those who lived with her, the depth of her prayer life, and many others. The fact that she did all this while starving for God's love in secret makes her life of faith all the more awe-inspiring. For myself, I am glad that the letters were preserved. They invite me to know the real Mother Teresa.

Mother succeeded in hiding her secret from her sisters and friends under the cloak of her smile. Some critics have suggested that in light of what we now know about her painful interior life, her cheerfulness was intended to deceive, just as she feared. She acknowledged as much to her confessor: "The whole time smiling.—Sisters and people pass such remarks.—They think my faith, trust and love are filling my very being and that the intimacy with God and union to His will must be absorbing my heart.—Could they but know—and how my cheerfulness is the cloak by which I cover the emptiness and misery."

Her cloak fooled me and others close to her. It also made us admire her all the more. "She knew how totally dependent she was on God for everything," said Sister Nirmala, ten years after Mother died. "She was fully aware of her limitations, her weaknesses, her helplessness, and her sinfulness. At the same time she knew how precious she was to God. And nothing or nobody could separate her from Him." Sister Nirmala was certain: "Mother did not doubt God, she continued to love Him. If you doubt someone, sooner or later you stop following Him. But she continued right up to her death to love Him and to put into practice her devotion."

In his book *Mother Teresa's Secret Fire* (2008), Father Joseph wrote, "Even more than to bring his comfort to the poor, God sent Mother Teresa *to be his light*. He invited her to pitch her tent in the blackest of places, not to build hospitals or high-rises, but that she might shine with his radiance." Mother Teresa's cheerfulness was rooted in her will and not in her feelings. She once explained, "Cheerfulness is a sign of a generous and mortified person who forgetting all things, even herself, tries to please her God in all she does for souls. Cheerfulness is often a cloak which hides a life of sacrifice. . . . For God loves a cheerful giver."

In April 1942, Mother had made a private vow to God "not to refuse him anything." It was her practice to "accept and offer" all that came her way. Whether God gave her illness or health, pain or comfort, sadness or joy, she would accept it and offer it back to God as her gift. About nine months before her death, in her 1996 Christmas letter, she acknowledged the health problems that had plagued her throughout the year, and her acceptance of them: "This year has been a gift of God for me. And I am happy that I have had something to give to Jesus also. We must take whatever He gives, and give whatever He takes with a big smile. . . . He loves us and knows what is best for us. I don't know why all this has happened this year, but I am sure of one thing— that Jesus does not make mistakes."

This simple philosophy guided her own approach to managing everything from an aching back to a hurting heart. A woman once brought her very sick ten-week-old baby to Mother Teresa and was desperate, sobbing, "I want my baby to live. I want this child." Mother calmly told her, "God has given you this great gift of life. If He wants you to give the gift back to Him, give it willingly, with love." The baby girl died five months later, and her mother felt Mother Teresa's words gave her strength to bear the loss demanded of her. She had learned to accept and offer.

Mother gave everything, and all she possessed in the end was the darkness of naked faith. "It often happens that those who spend their time giving light to others, remain in darkness themselves," she once explained to her sisters. For nearly fifty years, she accepted this as her lot, knowing the darkness would one day give way to eternal light, and she would be its carrier. "If I ever become a Saint," she wrote, "I will surely be one of 'darkness.' I will continually be absent from Heaven—to light the light of those in darkness on earth."

CHAPTER 13

Saying Goodbye

I prefer the insecurity of Divine Providence.

—*Mother Teresa*

On August 26, 1996, my son Maximilian was born. Mother had predicted the date, which was her eighty-sixth birthday. That same day, her heart failed, and she had to be shocked back to life. She was increasingly ill, with a heart and lungs that could not keep up with her relentless pace. Just a few days after Max's birth, Sister Priscilla called Sandy McMurtric from Calcutta to tell us Mother was still in the hospital and fading fast. Mary graciously allowed me to leave her with two toddlers and a newborn so that I could say goodbye. I met Sandy at Dulles airport outside Washington, and we flew on to Calcutta for a last farewell with the woman who had shown us the joy of a life lived for others.

Sister Priscilla greeted us with a grim update: "Mother isn't doing very well today. She is back on oxygen." When we arrived at the intensive care unit in Woodlands Hospital, there was a commotion among the sisters just outside Mother's room. I feared the worst. One of the sisters explained: "Mother was lying there on her bed, flat on her back, pointing her finger toward the ceiling. She couldn't talk because she had an oxygen mask on. We were all wondering what she was pointing at. Was a light out? Was she having a vision? And Mother saw our confusion and moved her mask to the side for a moment, and said, 'I'm going home. I'm going home to God.'"

We entered and went to Mother's bedside. She lay dressed in a blue-checkered hospital gown with a white cloth headpiece covering her hair and forehead. IV tubes and leads were tangled by her side, and she was pale from ten days in intensive care. Her rosary was firmly gripped in her hands.

Sandy greeted her first, and Mother was happy and surprised to see her. I was wearing a surgical mask and removed it for a moment so she could recognize me. "Oh, that you have come all this way to see me!" she said to us. "I am happy that you came."

I was eager to tell her my good news: "Mother, Mary had the baby on your birthday, just as you said. We have our third son."

She responded without a moment's hesitation, "Very good. But go home! Be with your family!"

Everyone in the room laughed. I had just traveled nine thousand miles, and Mother was already sending me away. I assured her that Mary was fine—my mom was with her—and I'd only be in Calcutta for a few days. She was satisfied. Then she lifted her head off the pillow, reached forward, and blessed my head with her left hand, since her right was immobilized by the IV tubes. I kissed her hand and said goodbye for the day.

For the next three days, I went to the private Mass that was celebrated in Mother's room each day at 6 a.m., just at the time it was said in the chapel at the motherhouse. The week before, Mother had requested (using a pen and paper because she was still on a ventilator) that the sisters bring her Holy Communion, and they had transformed her room into a chapel. Across from Mother's bed they had placed a small tabernacle where the Blessed Sacrament was reposed. Catholics believe that to be in the presence of the consecrated bread is to be in the presence of Jesus himself. It was covered by a white lace veil with a large medal depicting the infant Jesus, which Mother later gave to me for newborn Max.

To the side of the tabernacle, below a simple crucifix, two religious icons leaned against the wall. These were both favorites of Mother's: images of Mary as the "Immaculate Heart" and as "Our Lady of Guadalupe." At Mass each morning, I positioned myself so that I could observe her fervent devotion. She would fix her gaze upon the icons of Mary or the tabernacle. When it came time for Holy Communion, she strained to raise her head above the pillow to receive the host, as if she were going out to meet her Sacred Guest.

On my last day, Father Gary Duckworth, one of the founding MC Fathers, announced that he would be celebrating a Mass for the healing of the sick. "You mean for the dying?" Mother quipped. "Tell Him not to make me sick again!" At the close of the Mass, he administered the Sacrament of Anointing, what was once known as the last rites, to Mother. When I returned in the afternoon, she was much improved, sitting in a chair eating custard in a white habit with a rosary around her neck.

We talked about Mary and our three boys: James, Joseph, and Maximilian (four years, two years, and eight days old, respectively).

"One of them should become a priest," she said to me.

"Mother, if one of them becomes a priest, will you come to the ordination?"

Everyone laughed, including Mother. "Yes," she promised. "I will be there—either from heaven or on earth."

Two sisters shared with me that Mother had told the doctors that her "heart belonged to God," and she did not want any further medical treatments. She told the sisters, "If something is to happen to me, let it happen at home. I want to die naturally." Two days later, she was discharged and returned to the motherhouse. She was frail and forced to use a wheelchair much of the time, but she was home, where she could enjoy some privacy and uninterrupted rest.

My work for the past year had been with an advocacy group I had founded in Florida called Aging with Dignity. When my years trying to manage Florida's health and human services bureaucracy ended, I wanted to do something to influence the emerging national debate about doctor-assisted suicide and to improve end-of-life care. I talked with Mother about how I had learned from Kalighat and Gift of Peace that it is always easier to kill someone than care for them. She encouraged me to oppose assisted suicide by promoting hospice care and, more, to focus on the isolation and loneliness that is the curse of so many of the elderly poor and disabled.

To promote my new endeavor, Mother wrote an open letter of support urging people to help "defend and protect life, the most beautiful gift of God and to bring love and compassion to the elderly poor." "There are among us," she wrote, "so many who are poor and elderly, in need of understanding, respect, love and compassion, especially if they are sick, handicapped, helpless or alone. My prayer is that God may bless Jim and his beautiful work."

With the advice of hospice physicians, nurse practitioners, and chaplains, I created an advance care planning document called Five Wishes. It was inspired by my experiences at the Gift of Peace and Kalighat and what Mother had taught me about the dying. Like most end-of-life planning documents, it includes a living will and durable power of attorney for healthcare, to address the relevant legal issues. But it also covers pain management, comfort, dignity, and forgiveness. Five Wishes asks people to consider subjects like "What I want my loved ones to know" and "How I want to be remembered." It acknowledges that dying isn't just a medical moment but a deeply emotional and spiritual one—a truth to which Mother dedicated much of her life. Watching her age informed everything I have done at Aging with Dignity over the last twenty-five years.

Mother had her compass—her childlike faith in God—and the certainty that she was on an uninterrupted journey from God back to God. She prepared for her definitive departure from her beloved MC community and her joyful homecoming in the Father's house by means of a rigorous, disciplined prayer life that kept her in a perpetual state of readiness.

Prayer and action were inseparable for Mother Teresa. The work she did, the physical suffering and sense of abandonment by God she endured, the cheerfulness she exuded—all were part of abiding with the Lord. She experienced her own longing for God as a profound sense of thirst, just as he thirsted for souls. "I thirst"—Jesus's words to her on that train to Darjeeling—were inscribed on the side of the crucifix in every MC chapel throughout the world as a call to prayer and service for her sisters. The thirst of Christ was hers to satiate and experience. The author of Psalm 42 described this yearning:

As the hind longs for the running waters,
So my soul longs for you, O God.
Athirst is my soul for God, the living God.
When shall I go and behold the face of God?

Home at the motherhouse in September 1996, Mother slowly regained strength and returned to her daily routines. Ten weeks later she was back in intensive care at Woodlands. A bout of malaria and high fever had triggered another round of troubling heart symptoms. On November 22, she suffered a mild heart attack and was transferred to the BM Birla Heart Research Center. Doctors there reprogrammed her pacemaker, but her body was too weak for them to adequately treat her arrythmia. She also underwent an angioplasty procedure to remove blockages from two arteries and began to receive regular BiPap therapy for her badly compromised lungs—BiPaps are small ventilators that push air into your lungs while you wear a mask. Mother accepted these treatments but did not like them. Her kidneys, too, were beginning to fail. Mother's body was breaking down.

Calcutta's archbishop, Henry D'Souza, was convinced her spirit was in distress, too. Mother suffered from restlessness, disorientation, and insomnia during these weeks of hospitalization. At times she would thrash about in the bed, trying to pull off the heart-monitor leads attached to her body. Archbishop D'Souza feared she "might be under the attack of the evil one" and asked Father Rosario Stroscio, a Salesian priest, to pray over her that she be delivered from any diabolical attacks. Catholics call this an exorcism, though it holds little of the drama you find in the movies. His prayers did seem to calm her restlessness.

Only a few people were ever aware that this took place. Yet, in 2001, CNN ran a story, "Archbishop: Mother Teresa Underwent Exorcism" and implied she had been the victim of demonic possession. The confusion among the secular media was understandable. If one thinks a leprechaun as likely to exist as the devil, the distinction between being *tormented* and being *possessed* does not seem an important one. But the report caused an uproar. Archbishop D'Souza and Father Stroscio had to clarify that Mother Teresa was "not at all possessed by devils," and never had been. Sister Nirmala released a characteristically measured statement at the same time: "We are not at all sure whether she was really being disturbed by the devil or by her physical and psychological condition as she was so sick, and under heavy medication; and also, whether evil forces were trying to hinder Mother's medical treatment," she declared. "The devil cannot possess someone who is filled with God, and loves Him and all His children."

Mother certainly believed in the devil's active presence in the world. She had seen evil in the mortification of her beloved poor. In 1949, as she was setting out on her own, she wrote in her journal of how "the tempter" was attempting to weaken her resolve to found the MC. She once told me that she was bothered by what she had heard about Martin Scorsese's 1988 movie *The Last Temptation of Christ*. "So evil, this movie," she said, but "Evil," she went on, "is a test for greater love." Mother was unquestionably tested by it throughout her life. Her weaponry was faith, love, and service. Whether her alarming behavior in the hospital was caused by a bad reaction to medicine, low oxygen levels, or the torments of the devil—or some combination of the three—remains wrapped in mystery.

It was during Mother's stay in the Birla Center that I made the greatest mistake in all my years representing her and the MCs. I agreed to an interview with London's *Independent* newspaper. The reporter was married to my wife's maid of honor, and I felt I could trust him and wanted to help. We discussed Mother's health, and I shared with him my personal opinion that Mother was prepared to die and that some of the medical treatments she was receiving were against her will.

The headline the next day was "Mother Teresa Pleads with Her Friends: Just Let Me Die." I was quoted extensively. The story was inaccurate; there is a sharp distinction between being prepared to die and wanting to die. Nonetheless, my words upset some of the sisters. I apologized to Mother, the sisters, and the good doctors attending to Mother's care for my poor judgment in going on the record in the first place. Fortunately, they were focused on the vigil they were keeping by Mother's bedside and quickly moved past their disappointment with me. I am still mad at myself for the poor judgment I showed.

It was nearly Christmas, and after four weeks of hospitalization, Mother had had enough of hospital life. "Pack everything up—I am going home," she told Sister Nirmala Maria, an Irish MC and her nurse attendant. On December 19, that is precisely what they did.

Mother would need around-the-clock nursing at the motherhouse, so the MCs called Sister Roni. An American Benedictine nun, Sister Veronica Daniels had nursed Mother in both the United States and Calcutta on and off for a decade. When she first introduced herself as Roni, Mother looked askance and asked incredulously, "Your name is Veronica and you let them call you Roni?" Like us all, Sister Roni adored Mother.

In December 1996, she immediately flew to Calcutta, bringing along a BiPap breathing machine for the motherhouse. This was something impossible to procure at the time in India. "I had a long table outside her room for a desk, and at night, the sisters put a mattress on it for me to sleep," Sister Roni recalls. "I was with Mother from the time she got up until the time she went to bed. She was very frail, very human, lovely." Mother was happy to be spending Christmas in the company of those she loved the most—her MC family. She summoned the strength to give a Christmas blessing from the second-floor balcony to her sisters and guests assembled in the vast courtyard below her. Sister Roni stood next to the ailing nun in case she collapsed, but Mother's talk, filled with inspiration and scriptural references, went off without a hitch.

Roni Daniels stayed until February. Mother was stable, if little more. The full attention of the MCs and Mother was on preparations for the upcoming general chapter, a meeting of all the sisters held every six years to elect a superior general. In 1991, the sisters had failed to agree on a successor, and Mother reluctantly served another term. To her delight, on March 16, 1997, Sister Nirmala was chosen to replace her. Mother decided that she would personally introduce her successor to her friend Pope John Paul II in Rome. The May trip would have the added benefit of absenting Mother from the brutal heat that precedes the rainy season in Calcutta. (She had only recently agreed to have a fan placed in her room.)

When the day of departure arrived, Mother had a bad cold. Dr. Patricia Aubanel—a cardiologist from Tijuana who had treated Mother all around the world—worried that the trip was ill-advised, as Mother's heart and lungs seemed to be in a race to see which would fail first. Sister Gertrude, the second woman to join the MCs and herself a medical doctor, also disapproved of the idea. But Mother was adamant, and hers was the only vote that mattered. The doctors resigned themselves to her decision and boarded the airplane with medicines, oxygen, and a host of devices.

Sure enough, toward the end of the flight, Mother's health deteriorated rapidly. She had fits of coughing. She vomited. She struggled to breathe as her lungs began to fail her, and the doctors administered oxygen. Miraculously, by the time the plane landed in Rome, Mother had recovered enough to walk through part of the airport, waving to onlookers. The dream of passing the torch in Rome had seemingly kept her alive through it all. In June, Mother Teresa introduced Sister Nirmala to Pope John Paul II in a private audience. Mother was overjoyed that she could formally present her successor to the Holy Father. He asked whether Mother would retire now. All three laughed.

Mother had decided to carry on to a handful of final appointments in the United States. Few in her entourage agreed with the decision, but not even a phone call from Cardinal O'Connor of New York could dissuade her. Soon after arriving in New York City, she went by ambulance to an orthopedist who gave her a spinal epidural shot to allow her some relief from her back pain and to increase her mobility. Over the strong objections of Dr. Aubanel and Sister Gertrude, Mother then took the Delta shuttle to Washington that night, with her own oxygen tank in a seat nearby in case of an emergency.

On June 5, she went with Sandy McMurtrie and some of her sisters to the U.S. Capitol for a ceremony in the Rotunda where House Speaker Newt Gingrich and Senate president pro tempore Strom Thurmond presented her with the Congressional Gold Medal, the body's most prestigious civilian honor. She delivered brief remarks to the starstruck assembly of congressmen and women, thanking them for the honor. It would be her last public speech.

I missed the ceremony, but Mary, the children, and I spent time with Mother at Gift of Peace over the next three days. She seldom strayed from her wheelchair. The relief the epidural had given her was wearing off, and the unrelenting pain and advancing osteoporosis made for a crushing combination. Yet she smiled and played with the children, just as she had on previous visits. Mary asked her, "How can you be so cheerful when you are in such pain?" Mother replied, "I offer it all up."

For her return to New York, Sandy had arranged for a private plane to transport Mother because she could no longer sit for more than a few minutes at a time. Mother was loaded onto the plane on a stretcher, though she did manage to climb down the stairs to greet the sisters waiting for her in New York. Unlike in past visits to the Bronx, she had few appointments. Apart from her farewell visit, on June 18, with Princess Diana, Mother mostly rested.

On June 24, I had my last meeting with her. We needed to discuss the "NunBun" matter and also a Hallmark movie about her life that was in production. As she was wheeled into the convent parlor, she reached forward to greet me the way she always did, by placing her hands on both sides of my face and saying, "God bless you." But I had a bad case of conjunctivitis, so I backed away: "No, Mother, don't. I have pink eye, and it is very contagious." She grasped my face without hesitating. "Leprosy, AIDS, I don't get them." I should have known the woman who'd spent decades picking up lepers and holding TB patients as they died would never shrink from a bald guy with pink eye.

Knowing it could be my last opportunity, I thanked her for being a bridge between the rich and the poor. She was quiet for a moment, then said with a certain resignation, "And yet so few come and work with the poor. What will happen to the poor? Who will care for them?" And then she added, "I am going to the other side soon."

Our meeting had stretched for two hours, and finally one of her sisters placed her hands on the handles of Mother's wheelchair, my signal that the meeting was over. I asked Mother if she would stay a moment longer. My family had driven up with me as we knew it would be Mother's last trip to the United States. "Mother," I said, "before you go, Mary and the children are down in the courtyard. May they come up and receive your blessing?"

At the word "children," she stood up from her wheelchair and looked excitedly out the window in the direction of where they were playing. "Where are the children?" she asked. Sister Nirmala sent for them, and Mary and the boys came up immediately. She gave them all Miraculous Medals, and held each face for one last look of love. Mary and I kissed her hands and thanked her profusely.

After she had given each of us her blessing, we had begun to go down the stairs, when she called us back into the parlor. She had a gift: At her request, Sister Nirmala had removed the ceramic rendition of the Holy Family that had been hanging in Mother's room. Mother gave it to us to hang in our family home.

I have thought many times over the years of the expression on Mother's face when she looked out the window in search of my children. It was filled with the joy and peace of a life lived for others. She had prayed, "Jesus, meek and humble of heart, make my heart like unto Thine," and her prayer had been answered.

On her way home to Calcutta, Mother Teresa stopped one last time in Rome, where she saw the Holy Father twice. Their first visit took place at the Pallium Mass he presided over in Saint Peter's Basilica. It transpired, appropriately enough for the pope and missionary, on the feast of Saints Peter and Paul. The Holy Father detoured from his recessional route to walk over to Mother and embrace her. She was in her wheelchair but rose when he approached. His hands shook slightly from the Parkinson's disease that would hasten his death eight years later. Their spiritual bond and grateful affection were beautifully human, as well as deeply sacred, and the photo of them as they embraced showed unmistakably the tenderness and friendship between these two future saints.

Their second and final meeting occurred about two weeks later in the Holy Father's private office. Sister Nirmala and Sister Nirmala Maria accompanied her. "Wheel me in!" Mother said playfully as they left the ornate waiting area. Mother was positioned directly across from John Paul. After a brief exchange of pleasantries, the Holy Father sat down and stared at Mother. He nodded his head knowingly and said, simply, "I thirst."

The pope truly understood her like no one else. He knew that these words of Jesus from the cross were the theological inspiration for everything Mother Teresa had done in the nearly fifty years since she had left the comfortable confines of the Loreto cloister. He knew it was not social work that she had performed in the streets of Calcutta. Her deeds were, as she often put it, her way "to satiate the thirst of Christ for love and souls."

It was time for Mother to say goodbye to the shepherd who seemed to be her soul mate on earth. She bent to kiss his papal ring, and he stooped over to embrace her. She later asked Sister Nirmala Maria, "Did he kiss my head?" and was delighted to learn that he had. Of all the honors and recognition that she experienced in her life, none meant more to her than the fact that the successor to Saint Peter personally cared so much about her.

When she arrived in Calcutta on July 22, she was welcomed at the airport by a group of sisters who were the closest to her, as well as her longtime personal physician, Dr. Alfred Woodward. She greeted him saying, "Now my work is done."

CHAPTER 14

Going Home

Death is something beautiful: it means going home.

—*Mother Teresa*

Hanging on the wall in Kalighat is a placard that reads, "The Greatest Aim Of Human Life Is To Die In Peace With God—Mother." For many years, it was the only one of Mother's ideas I didn't believe in absolutely. Having peace of mind and tranquility at the moment of death is a worthy goal, but it never struck me as something to build a life around. It didn't even appear to be *her* greatest aim. She frequently spoke of the pursuit of holiness, of choosing heaven, of becoming a saint, as the highest callings.

It took years for me to understand that the "peace" she described wasn't a destination or state of mind, but rather a pursuit, a way of life. She eventually taught me that the best way to *die* at peace with God was to learn how to *live* at peace with Him, as an individual and as a member of the human family. Put another way, Mother saw life as one long preparation for the thing that her parents asked for her in their prayers at her baptism: eternal life.

People of all faiths have struggled for millennia with how to describe "eternal life." When he was nine, my son Joe brought the problem home to me. We were driving back from Sunday Mass, and he was complaining about how long it had gone on. Mary mused: "In heaven, we won't just spend an hour, we will spend eternity praising and thanking God." Joe sulked in the back seat: "That isn't much to look forward to."

Pope Benedict XVI recognized this conundrum in his 2007 encyclical "Saved in Hope." "To live always, without end," he observed, would be "monotonous and ultimately unbearable." Rather than "an unending succession of days in the calendar," he suggested eternity would be "something more like the supreme moment of satisfaction, in which totality embraces us and we embrace totality." He likened it to "plunging into the ocean of infinite love, a moment in which time—the before and after—no longer exists."

I'm not sure a plunge into the "ocean of infinite love" would have satisfied the nine-year-old Joe, but it aligns perfectly with Mother Teresa's conception of coming from and going home to God. Love was her vocation. "We were created by God for great things, to love and be loved," she said regularly, both in speeches and in conversation. She felt that to love and be loved was more important than the material requirements of life; more important than food, shelter, or clothing.

For her, heaven was a social reality, a communion of persons in God. She often spoke of how she longed to see her mother, her sister, and her brother in heaven, to be with them for eternity. She rejected the idea that there was a class structure to heaven, where the spiritually elite resided in one sphere, separated from the rest of the elect. "One thing I am sure of is that there aren't levels in heaven like that," she told Sandy McMurtrie one day when they were on a car trip. Mother saw heaven as a restoration of the perfect unity of God and man that had been established at the time of creation and was broken by the Fall of Adam and Eve. This was the home she sought her whole life.

Such a sphere of being is beyond our finite minds to conceive or communicate. Nonetheless, Mother Teresa believed "the kingdom of God" could be experienced, albeit imperfectly, in this life through the brief moments of sublime wonder that all encounter at some point on their journey. I remember one early morning in Washington when a mother brought her infant to Mother Teresa to bless. She looked into the baby's eyes and stroked her tiny head as if she were beholding the face of God. Here was an "ocean of infinite love." A foretaste of the kingdom to come seemed to immerse Mother in that moment.

Henry Francis Lyte's hymn "Abide with Me" captures Mother's experience of this life and expectation of the next. (I first heard it at Mother's funeral mass, where a choir of sisters sang it as her body was carried from the arena.) The words of the first and last verses speak perfectly of her heart's longing:

Abide with me: fast falls the eventide;
The darkness deepens; Lord with me abide.
When other helpers fail and comforts flee,
Help of the helpless, O abide with me.

Hold thou thy cross before my closing eyes.
Shine through the gloom and point me to the skies.
Heaven's morning breaks, and earth's vain shadows flee.
In life, in death, O Lord, abide with me.

The deepening darkness and gloom, the flight of comfort, and the shadows of her own approaching mortality did not seem to frighten or concern Mother in the least. She awaited her death the way one might a postal delivery, keeping a watchful eye out while consuming herself with her missionary activities. She seemed ready to leave this world on a minute's notice. Her health had long been precarious; during the years I knew her, she had nearly died almost a dozen times from heart attacks, pneumonia, and malaria. Every time we said goodbye I wondered if I would ever see her again. On one occasion in 1995, I said farewell for what I thought would be the last time, and she replied, matter-of-factly, "I have my bags packed."

Though Mother had her bags packed, her sisters were not going to let her go without a fight. By September 1997, they had stocked the motherhouse with a vast array of emergency medical supplies and equipment. Sister Dominga, who joined in the early 1980s and had become a leader within the MCs, put it very bluntly: "If God wants to get Mother, He better come when she's alone."

That would be no easy task. The sisters doted on Mother day and night. She had always been the giver and the servant, had always sacrificed for them. But as her body failed and she was increasingly incapacitated, Mother became more and more dependent on her sisters. And this reversal of roles was an unmissable opportunity for them to return love for love.

Now they could grasp her hand and kiss it. Now they could help her get dressed in the morning and again at night. Meals were brought to her room. Masses were celebrated at her bedside when her health demanded. Sisters helped her to bed early and encouraged her not to be the first in the chapel in the morning. They took special care to manage her vast array of medicines, and vied over who was allowed to push her wheelchair. The sisters delighted in spoiling their Mother.

Four sisters were particularly focused on caring for Mother in her last weeks. Sister Gertrude was the most senior of the sisters since Sister Agnes's death in April 1997. Mother had tapped her to go to medical school during the first years of the MCs, to be able to provide medical care for the dying at Kalighat. Mother Teresa had now become her patient. Sister Gertrude alternated in nursing and accompanying Mother these last days with Sister Shanti, also a physician, and Sister Luke, the longtime superior of Kalighat. And tirelessly helping and seeing to Mother's every need was Sister Nirmala Maria. She had been a Loreto sister before following Mother's footsteps to the motherhouse in 1989, and had frequently traveled with Mother during her last years. She was now responsible for getting her reluctant charge to swallow more than a dozen pills each day and with administering the daily BiPap machine breathing therapies. The daily battle of wills over BiPap treatments required resourcefulness. Mother consented as long as it was paired with saying the rosary, and Sister Nirmala Maria added extra Hail Marys to prolong the sessions.

During the last weeks of her life, in August and September 1997, Mother reveled in the company of her sisters like never before. Her last supper with her sisters was on a Wednesday, September 3, two days before she died. She tried to abandon her privileged place at the table in deference to her successor, but Sister Nirmala would not allow it. Mother could never be just an ordinary sister. The evening featured Mother's favorite custard dish, prepared specially for her by the MCs who lived and worked at an orphanage a half mile away from the motherhouse. She got a generous serving and enjoyed it immensely. Mother's sweet tooth was forever young.

The custard would be the last dessert she would enjoy. Her health took a turn for the worse that evening. Around 10 p.m., she became quite ill, vomiting and spending most of the next six hours in the bathroom. Her blood pressure spiked to 200/80. Her back pain, which she referred to as "her old friend," returned with a vengeance.

By 4 a.m., she was finally able to sleep. She was too exhausted to go for prayer in the chapel with her sisters at 6 a.m., but she had Mass celebrated in her room at 11 a.m. In the afternoon, at the teatime that followed lunch and siesta, the sisters brought her a little food, which she ate, and afterward Father Mervyn Carapiet came and heard what would be her last confession. Whatever penance he may have given Mother Teresa could not have been more punishing than her back pain. The pain medicine and the hot water bottles the sisters applied to her back were no match for her "old friend's" wrath. Because she had slept so little the previous night, Mother finished a light dinner and went to bed soon after.

The Gospels meticulously describe Christ's passion and death, just as Scripture recounts the last acts and conversations of Moses, David, Elijah, and other prophets. Catholics have honored this tradition and recorded in detail the deaths of the saints, including their final words and actions, to give witness to their holiness and encourage the faithful.

September 5, 1997, fell on what the MCs commemorate as a "first Friday." Since the late seventeenth century, the Catholic Church has promoted special devotion to the Sacred Heart of Jesus on the first Friday of every month, accompanied by penitential practices, to commemorate his infinite love and mercy and make reparations for sin. For the MCs, this means a special one-hour prayer vigil in the chapel until midnight on Thursday, as well as fasting at lunch the next day.

Mother Teresa awoke that first Friday fully expecting to follow the disciplinary practices of the religious community she'd built. But her back continued to bedevil her, and she couldn't attend morning prayers. As Sister Nirmala Maria helped her dress for Mass, she gave her some painkillers to relieve enough of her suffering so she could make it to the chapel with the other sisters. At the conclusion of Mass, Sister Luke wheeled her out to meet a couple from Bombay who had tried for days to get a private visit and photo with Mother. It was Mother's practice to greet any visitor to the motherhouse who asked to see her, though she never ceased to dislike being photographed and claimed that every time she had her picture taken, a soul was released from purgatory. No one can count how many souls escaped to heaven thanks to Mother's patience.

Mother returned to her room for a breakfast of tea, bread, and a banana. Immediately after, she had her first BiPap treatment of the day, which took the length of a rosary. She then plunged into work. First, she convened a special meeting of the MC council, the governing group of five sisters elected by their peers, at 9 a.m. After this hour session, she went to her desk and began signing forms authorizing women to take temporary or final vows as MCs. She also signed all the correspondence prepared by Sister Joel, Mother's secretary who had worked closely with her for fifteen years. Mail had piled up because Mother had not been able to do desk work for several days. She insisted that she personally sign her own letters and acknowledgments of donations, just as she had always done. She bent to the task and then, just like a proud schoolgirl after completing an assignment, carried the box of signed correspondence from her room to Sister Joel's desk in the main office.

Seeing Mother Teresa back to her old routines after having had such a dreadful day surprised and reassured her sisters. Sister Nirmala Maria then brought Mother a medicinal drink for her kidneys, heart, and lungs.

It was now around 1 p.m., and Mother went to the chapel for midday prayer. At its conclusion, she heard the footsteps of a little boy running in the passageway outside the chapel, and she happily said to Sister Nirmala Maria, "I think there is someone waiting for me outside." The boy was a four-year-old whose grandmother had brought a friend with her daughter to meet Mother. They had an impromptu gathering in the same greeting area where I first met Mother. The daughter was depressed and had contemplated suicide, and she and her mother asked Mother to pray that this mental disturbance would leave her. Mother happily agreed. These visitors would be the last to receive Mother's signature hands-on-the-head blessing.

Normally, Mother would have gone on to lunch, but because of the first Friday fast, she did not want to eat. She had spent a lifetime scrupulously following the schedule and rules of her religious congregation and was not about to deviate. She knew the power of leading by example, so when it came to the question of fasting or not, she was adamant that she should not be excused from the sacrifices that the other sisters were making. When the sisters tried to wheel her chair into a room where lunch awaited her, she reached out and grabbed the walls of the doorway to prevent her own passage. Finally, Sister Nirmala came and reminded Mother that it was her own long-standing policy in the motherhouse that all sick sisters had to eat lunch on first Fridays. Only then did Mother acquiesce. This may have been one battle that she happily lost; she was hungry after eating so little the day before. She had rice and salad from the dishes brought to her desk and then retired for her midday siesta.

When she awoke, her back pain was again excruciating. She took her tea in bed, leaning on an elbow. Afterward, she arose and sat at her table doing spiritual reading, just as the MC daily schedule provided. The sky had gone dark outside, and a storm soon followed. Sister Nirmala Maria closed Mother's window and turned on a light so she could continue to read. She also urged Mother to return to her bed because sitting was bad for her back, but Mother resisted. It took Sister Nirmala's gentle encouragement to get her to obey. Another BiPap treatment and rosary with Sister Nirmala Maria followed.

Mother Teresa submitted to the hated treatment, then she arose from bed as if on a mission, saying that she had not finished all the correspondence Sister Joel had prepared for her. Her mood had improved, and she laughed when Sister Nirmala Maria joked that Mother was busier now than when she was superior general. Nothing was going to stop Mother from clearing her desk that Friday. She signed thank-you notes to donors until around 4:30 p.m.

With her work finished, she returned to her room. Brother Geoff, the head of the Missionaries of Charity Brothers, had come to the motherhouse to say goodbye to Mother before he departed for a trip to Singapore. The sisters who guarded Mother felt that such visits sapped her energy, but because Brother Geoff was part of their family, they knew they had to relent. He met with Mother in her room and departed with a gift he still cherishes. Mother had given him a framed image of the Sacred Heart of Jesus that she herself had frequently venerated during her BiPap treatments.

Mother's back pain had worsened during the meeting, though. The pain pills were not providing relief. Sister Nirmala Maria shared her concerns with Sister Shanti, who approved giving her Lodine—a stronger anti-inflammatory drug—which a doctor had prescribed for Mother when she was in New York three months earlier.

Shortly after 5 p.m., Mother Teresa was wheeled to the entrance of her room so she could wave to the Bollywood actress Shashikala, who was standing on the chapel verandah, hoping to get a glimpse of the future saint. But sitting had become so painful that Mother was forced immediately to return to her bed. Sister Shanti had Mother lie on her right side while she massaged her back, pressing hard through a pillow so as not to injure the fragile nun's spine or brittle bones. Mother exhorted her to rub more aggressively. "Hard pressure on that spot," she directed, and Sister Shanti complied. "Lovely," Mother responded. As Sister Shanti administered the massage, she prayed the rosary with Mother, who often could not even respond to the prayers so great was her pain.

Sister Gertrude had been away most of the day and returned around this time. Mother said to her in mock seriousness, "You left me!" Sister Gertrude explained that she had been out at Prem Dan, one of the MC missions. Then Mother told her, "My old friend came back," referring to her back pain. But Mother also seemed disoriented. Three times she said to Sister Gertrude, "Come, let us go home." Sister Gertrude gently corrected her: "But Mother, we are home."

Throughout this illness, as well as all those that preceded it, Mother Teresa tried to offer up her pain to God. She prayed while she suffered and had images above her bed to help her focus: one of Mary, the Mother of Jesus; a photo of Saint Thérèse of Lisieux with the quote "My Vocation is Love"; the image of the Sacred Heart; and a small crown of thorns, with a cross in the middle. On this final night of her life, she had plenty of pain to offer up. The Lodine was not having its intended effect, and Mother's pain remained excruciating. Sister Gertrude saw her kiss an image of Jesus crowned with thorns, which she always interpreted as Mother identifying with his agony and sorrow. Mother passed some of the late afternoon listening to Sister Gertrude read from *Only Jesus* by Luis Martínez, the first archbishop of Mexico City, a book that was by her bedside.

At 6 p.m., it was time for the community of MCs to gather in the chapel for Eucharistic adoration. Even though Mother wanted to go, the sisters insisted she stay in bed and not aggravate her back further. She prayed a rosary with Sister Nirmala Maria, and then spoke on the phone with her friend Sunita Kumar. Sunita had called to ask for prayers for her son, Arjun, who had just been diagnosed with hepatitis C. During their conversation Mother made no mention of how poorly she felt. At the conclusion of holy hour in the chapel, Sister Nirmala brought the pyx containing the Blessed Sacrament to Mother, who reverently and tenderly kissed it, as if it were a last goodbye. Mother then had a sandwich for dinner in her room and prepared to return to her bed.

The storm had only gotten worse. The sky was pitch-black, and the wind howled as Mother got into her night-clothes and put on baby powder as was her custom during the more humid months. The temperature in her room dropped as the storm front moved in, and Mother grew cold. "Cover me with the blanket you brought from Rome," she asked Sister Gertrude. The wool blanket had sentimental value for both of them. Sister Gertrude had given it to Mother in Taizé, France, in 1976 at an interfaith gathering where thousands of young people had prayed for peace. It had long been one of Mother's favorites, but she had left it at the MC house in Rome. Sister Gertrude had only recently brought it back to Calcutta for her.

A violent storm was now pounding the city. Electrical storms strike Calcutta with astonishing ferocity. I was stunned the first time I experienced one, even after growing up with Florida's hurricanes and daily thunderstorms. In Calcutta, the lightning strikes come in rapid succession and are blinding. The claps of thunder ricochet off the concrete buildings and streets, making a late-summer electrical storm sound like the London Blitz.

The storm heralded the beginning of the end for Mother. She suddenly couldn't breathe. As she sat on the edge of the bed gasping for air, Sister Gertrude checked her vital signs, growing more and more worried about her lungs. "Mother is drowning in her own secretions," she quietly told the other sisters. Everyone raced to get the emergency medical equipment and supplies they had stored for this moment, hoping to mechanically assist Mother's failing lungs and heart.

At the very moment when this equipment might have made a difference, a magnificent bolt of lightning struck the neighborhood and triggered an unprecedented power failure in the motherhouse. This was no ordinary power outage. Electricity interruptions in the Calcutta convent were common, but on this night, not only did the main electrical line stop working but the backup line the sisters depended on for emergencies also went down.

It was now about 8:30 p.m. and the motherhouse was dark. Sisters scrambled for candles, but had to be careful around Mother's cannister of oxygen, which supplied a mostly futile nose clip attached to Mother. Sister Shanti commanded that someone summon Dr. Woodward, who had come to the motherhouse on many previous occasions to attend to Mother in extremis. He and his wife, a nurse, dropped everything to rush over.

Sister Joel also ran to the office and called the nearest

parish, Saint Mary's—where Mother Teresa's original work with the poor of Calcutta began—to get a priest to come immediately to administer the last rites. Father Hansel D'Souza happened to be sitting near the phone awaiting a friend's call when Sister Joel reached him. He was just minutes from the motherhouse and immediately on his way.

The sisters, meanwhile, were doing their best to attend to their restless, dying mother. The pulse oximeter was battery-operated, but the numbers it displayed for Sister Nirmala Maria confirmed that Mother's situation was dire. On her recent flight from Calcutta to Rome, her reading of 85 had been cause for alarm; it was now below 50. Her pulse, normally around 90, was horribly irregular, reading 55 then 130 then 200. Mother Teresa sat on the edge of her bed, her eyes bulging from her battle for air.

It was clear to all that Mother Teresa's life was slipping away, her heart and lungs both failing. Sister Luke struggled to sort through the emergency drugs with her small flashlight. The BiPap machine, which could have assisted her breathing and possibly extended her life, was sitting nearby, useless without electricity.

Mother spoke her last audible words at around 8:45 p.m.: "I can't breathe." It was such a natural, normal thing to say under the circumstances. The storm outside raged unabated, yet a relative calm descended on Mother. She was surrounded by her beloved sisters. They did all they could do to make her comfortable, assuring her that a priest and Dr. Woodward were on the way. As they waited together in the candlelit darkness, they poured out their love in tears and anxious prayers.

Father D'Souza arrived first and immediately gave Mother the last rites, anointing her with sacramental oils reserved for such an occasion. She was conscious throughout. Dr. Woodward arrived just after her anointing, and began his preparations to administer drugs and intubate her in the dark, crowded room. The sisters thronged Mother's bed, reciting prayers that she had taught them to pray: "Sacred Heart of Jesus, I trust in you" and "Mary, Mother of Jesus, be a mother to Mother now." According to Sister Gertrude, who held Mother's head in her lap, her lips appeared to move with these prayers; her lips also seemed to repeat "Jesus," over and over. Her voice was not audible because her lungs were no longer working.

It had only been five to ten minutes in darkness, but it had seemed interminable. When the lights came back on, the crowded room became chaotic as everyone scrambled to help. The sisters gave Mother an injection of Deriphyllin to help her breathe and another of Lasix to address the fluid buildup in her lungs, part of the emergency procedure they already had in place. Then the power went off again, this time for two minutes, exasperating the distraught sisters. They could not depend on any of their medical interventions. Nature would take its course, unimpeded.

Mother's head still rested in Sister Gertrude's lap as the sisters continued their prayers and exhortations to God. At 8:57 p.m., Mother Teresa looked to the side, then up, then closed her eyes. She never opened them again. She had commended her soul to the One who had created her and breathed life into her these eighty-seven years. She had died in her own bed, surrounded by her sisters, just as she'd wanted.

Dr. Woodward did what doctors are trained to do at such a moment; he attempted to revive Mother. He intubated her, administered an emergency injection in her femoral artery, and performed a heart massage. The oximeter to which she was connected registered a heartbeat, which gave the sisters in the room a brief glimmer of hope. But the heartbeat it detected was from the pacemaker that had been implanted years earlier. Dr. Woodward soon realized that this time there would be no revival. Mother had already gone home to God. She was in the Father's house, secure, peaceful, triumphant, free.

At 9:30 p.m., Dr. Woodward said to Sister Nirmala, "Mother has gone to Jesus." He unhooked her from the machines and declared her dead.

Mother had been on the brink of death so many times before—Dr. Woodward later estimated ten to twelve times—and had always rallied. The thunder they had heard crashing through Calcutta now would be remembered as blasts of celestial trumpets announcing the arrival of a faithful servant. Heaven had waited long enough.

Sister Nirmala announced the news of Mother's death to the 250 novices gathered in prayer in the chapel directly across from Mother's room. A loud cry spontaneously arose from among them. Sister Immacula, a sister who was with the novices, said it was a wailing that would have broken the hardest heart. The combination of the bizarre power outages with the confirmation of their worst fears overwhelmed Mother's spiritual daughters.

And yet, Sister Nirmala said, it was impossible not to think of Mother standing before the throne of God and hearing the very words of Jesus that she had quoted on countless occasions during her life: "'Come, you whom my Father has blessed, take for your heritage the kingdom prepared for you since the foundation of the world. For I was hungry and you gave me food; I was thirsty and you gave me drink; I was a stranger and you made me welcome; naked and you clothed me, sick and you visited me, in prison and you came to see me.' Then the virtuous will say to him in reply, 'Lord, when did we see you hungry and feed you; or thirsty and give you drink? When did we see you a stranger and make you welcome; naked and clothe you; sick or in prison and go to see you?' And the King will answer, 'I tell you solemnly, in so far as you did this to one of the least of these brothers of mine, you did it to me.'"

CHAPTER 15

Saint Teresa of Calcutta

By blood, I am Albanian. By citizenship, an Indian. By faith, I am a Catholic nun. As to my calling, I belong to the world. As to my heart, I belong entirely to the heart of Jesus.

—*Mother Teresa*

Pope John Paul II spoke for all of us in the days after Mother Teresa's death. At his first public appearance after he learned the news, he broke from his prepared remarks to speak in a shaking voice of her "luminous example" and embrace of "the hearts of the dying, of the abandoned children, of the men and women crushed by the weight of suffering and solitude." At Mass the following day, he recalled his friend with affection: "She lives in my memory as a tiny figure, whose entire existence was the service of the poorest of the poor, but who was always full of an inexhaustible spiritual energy, the energy of the love of Christ." Her death, he would say later, "left us all a little orphaned."

That was certainly how I felt. I was on a business trip in the Tampa Bay area, heading for the airport and a flight home to Tallahassee. I had stopped at a gas station to top off my rental car when I got a 911 message on my pager from Jackie Roberts, my assistant at Aging with Dignity. I found the pay phone and called Jackie, who told me the Associated Press was confirming that Mother had died. I burst into tears.

I was surprised by the depth of my reaction to news I had long expected. Mother was eighty-seven, truly ancient for Calcutta. She had spent every drop of herself every day and been so ill for so long. I had called the motherhouse two days earlier, and Sister Priscilla said Mother was fine, up and about doing her work. But now the defining chapter of my life was over. Is it any wonder I couldn't stop crying out front of a 7-Eleven at the Tampa airport?

Yet Mother's friends here on earth still had work to do. Just a few weeks after her death, the pope was already expressing his hope that she would be canonized. He fast-tracked the process by which the Catholic Church pronounces someone a saint by waiving most of the five-year waiting period required to even begin formal consideration. I was one of 113 people asked by the Vatican to testify under oath as part of their assessment of her worthiness to join the ranks of the elect.

Father Brian Kolodiejchuck and Sister Lynn from the motherhouse led a team of MCs charged with preparing the documentation needed by the Vatican to scrutinize her case. Within two years, they had assembled eighty-three volumes containing thirty-five thousand pages of documents, beginning with her baptismal certificate, and submitted them to the Vatican's Congregation for the Causes of Saints. I contributed to this file, submitting a fifty-six-page statement and a further forty-one exhibits, including legal correspondence, memoranda to Mother, and nine handwritten letters from her.

Mary and I were the unintended beneficiaries of this stem-to-stern sweep of files and records at the motherhouse. In June 2000, we received a packet from Calcutta. It included a photo of our family that I had sent to Mother years earlier. In her letter, Sister Priscilla wrote:

> Enclosed a real treasure, which we found the other day in a drawer of Mother's desk. We had never gone into her desk before—so 2½ years later we found this photograph! Can you imagine? Mother never kept photographs or indeed, anything! And she kept this! I am sure you will treasure it!

It felt like a message from beyond the grave.

I had been back to Calcutta a couple of times and prayed at Mother's tomb on the ground floor of the motherhouse. It had become a tourist destination and place of pilgrimage, and each day, thousands of visitors paid their respects. MC sisters were often among them. Even though their Christian beliefs assured them that she was closer to them than before, they missed her physical presence terribly.

But they carried on the work she had begun, and they saw fresh signs of God's favor. In the first year after Mother's death, eleven houses were opened, in India, Africa, South America, and the Middle East. Within ten years, 1,000 new sisters and more than 150 new homes were added as the MCs expanded their reach from 120 to 134 countries.

Meanwhile, Mother Teresa's cultural power did not wane. Numerous documentaries, and even a feature-length movie, were produced. One of the best was Ann and Jan Petrie's *The Legacy*, a follow-up to their original masterpiece that included footage from the funeral and interment. Innumerable books and magazine articles were published about Mother and her works. The U.S. Postal Service issued a commemorative postage stamp to honor her.

My life after Mother became, by necessity, more serious and purposeful than before. While she lived, I was safe in her protective bubble, and it had been unthinkable for me to do anything that would in the slightest way tarnish my relationship with her. I adapted Saint Paul's exhortation to the people of Corinth—"Imitate me as I imitate Christ"—and tried in my own way to imitate Mother. My Christian life had taken root in her shadow, and with her gone, I now had to choose to either put her teachings and example into practice or squander the graces I had received and revert to the spiritual mediocrity I had known.

Fortunately, her fresh memory and my good wife made this no choice at all. And besides, I had promised Mother when she was in the intensive care unit at Woodlands that I would continue to help the MCs after she was gone. That pledge sufficed to keep me engaged in the work, and there was always plenty to be done with the MCs, for as Jesus said, "The poor you will always have with you."

I continued policing fraudulent fundraising efforts and unauthorized uses of Mother's name. A motivational poem, "Do It Anyway," was attributed to her and reproduced on posters and prayer cards, though it was actually written by

Kent Keith. The tabloid *Weekly World News* ran a cover story called "The End Times Prophecies of Mother Teresa," which claimed to be based on her "deathbed predictions." These included famine, widespread cannibalism, a civil war in the United States, forty days and forty nights of blood-red rain, and on Christmas Day 1998, the birth of "a new Christ Child" in Canada. All bogus, of course.

While such news items attracted little interest, the Vatican's announcement in 2002 that Mother Teresa was officially on the road to sainthood did. The Catholic Church's process for canonization requires the intermediate step of "beatification"—a formal finding by the Vatican that confirms both the candidate's "heroic virtue" and a miracle attributed to his or her intercession with God. To be a miracle under Church criteria, an event has to involve the healing of an individual that was immediate, complete, and had no scientific explanation, and followed a specific appeal to the saint's intercession. The Congregation for the Causes of Saints and its panel of medical specialists certify all such events.

It had taken less than six years for these boxes to be checked—unheard of speed in Rome. This accelerated approval was possible because of an Indian woman in West Bengal whose large abdominal tumor disappeared within hours of praying for Mother's intercession. After this miracle was certified, Pope John Paul II wasted no time in scheduling a public ceremony to honor his friend and move her another step closer to sainthood.

To underscore the importance of Mother Teresa to him personally, he chose to have the beatification ceremony coincide with the twenty-fifth anniversary of his elevation to the papacy. A series of weekend activities, including an orchestral concert, were planned to honor the ailing pontiff and his towering accomplishments, but all was to culminate on Sunday in the official recognition of Mother Teresa's sanctity. The pope surely wished to deflect attention from himself as well as honor a woman he admired. The United States sent a presidential delegation led by President George W. Bush's sister-in-law, first lady of Florida Columba Bush. The president, my boss at the time, asked me to be a member of this group, which also included prominent U.S. Catholics such as a former ambassador to the Holy See, Jim Nicholson; the political commentator Peggy Noonan; and the Harvard Law professor Mary Ann Glendon.

When the day of the Mass of Beatification came, Saint Peter's Square was packed with around three hundred thousand people. Pope John Paul was wheeled out of the Basilica and onto the plaza in a mobile chair specially designed to accommodate his increasing disability from Parkinson's disease. He knew he would not live to see Mother canonized, so he held back nothing in his acclaim of his friend, calling her "an icon of the Good Samaritan." "Let us praise the Lord," he exhorted the crowd, "for this diminutive woman in love with God, a humble Gospel messenger and tireless benefactor of humanity."

All that remained for her to go from "Blessed" to "Saint" Teresa of Calcutta was a second miracle that passed muster with the Vatican. Father Brian's office was swamped with thousands of accounts of extraordinary blessings—what Vatican experts call "favors" instead of true miracles—attributed to Mother's intercession. I experienced my own favor in 2009.

I was president of Saint Vincent College in Pennsylvania and had suspended one of the Benedictine priest-professors and notified law enforcement after I was presented with convincing evidence that the monk had viewed child pornography on the university's network. The priest's defense was that a student had used his computer without his knowledge to access the objectionable material. He claimed he only accepted his suspension in order to protect the student, who had admitted this sin during confession.

The campus was convulsed in controversy, and many on the faculty and among the student body were convinced I had ruined an innocent man. I knew better because data retrieved from a keystroke-logging program pointed to the professor and not the student, but it was hard for me to prove he was lying with the largely circumstantial evidence I had. The priest had created such an uproar that I announced I would leave my position at the end of the academic year to prevent this sideshow from distracting students from their education.

The turmoil at the college was taking its toll on me, and I decided to drive four hours to Washington to be with the MCs for the profession of final vows that took place every December for new groups of sisters. Being around the MCs always refreshed my soul, and I needed nothing less. When I arrived at the Basilica of the Immaculate Conception where the Mass was to be held, I went downstairs to where a large statue of Mother Teresa stands. I knelt beneath it and poured out my heart to her, insisting that it could not be God's plan for this priest to be vindicated when I knew that he was guilty. I wept before Mother's statue like I had before her body in Saint Thomas Church more than a decade earlier.

After I finished my prayer, I went upstairs for the Mass and, afterward, visited with some sisters I hadn't seen in years. With my spirits renewed, I headed home.

Somewhere along the Pennsylvania turnpike, I received a phone call from Dennis Grace, my right-hand man at the college, who had urgent news: Eddie Dejthai, the college's chief information officer, had recovered from the college's databases a number of highly incriminating personal photos and emails that the priest thought he had deleted. This was the indisputable proof I needed. I turned it all over to the Vatican. While it still took several years, the Congregation for the Doctrine of the Faith, relying heavily on the evidence unearthed by Eddie that December day, defrocked the priest and expelled him from monastic life. Pope Benedict himself signed the final order.

All of this happened, I am convinced, thanks to Mother's intercession. As with the miracles in the time of Christ, one can explain away as coincidence the mysterious appearance of conclusive proof against the deviant priest just hours after I prayed to Mother. Though the Catholic Church officials overseeing Mother's canonization process would call it a favor, it was to me a bona fide miracle.

In December 2008, a man in Brazil with numerous abscesses in his brain had fallen into a coma and was not expected to live. His wife prayed to Mother Teresa, desperately pleading for his recovery, placing a relic on the side of his head where the tumors were. As surgeons prepared for a last-ditch operation to relieve pressure on his brain, the man awoke and asked, "What am I doing here?" The abscesses were gone. He was fully recovered. It was a miracle. And seven years later, it was official; the Vatican had recognized its second miracle.

Pope Francis immediately scheduled the canonization ceremony, and about six months later, I received a phone call from Calcutta. It was Sister Lynn, one of the MCs in charge of the preparations for the event. She called to convey a request from their new superior general: "Sister Prema would like for you to do the first reading at the Mass of Canonization for Mother."

I said yes, thanked God, and called Mary. But I was a bit numb—I didn't deserve this privilege any more than I deserved to be Mother's friend in the first place. I thought of all the other people closer to her who merited this honor, and even more, the MC sisters, brothers, and fathers who had labored by her side.

But I wasn't going to second guess fate. To me, the request to do the reading at the Mass of Canonization came from on high with Mother Teresa's blessing if not orchestration. She knew how grateful I was that she had permitted me to enter into her confidence and become her friend, and this new privilege would simply add to these blessings.

In September 2016, Rome was in the midst of a heat wave, and the unseasonable weather made the city feel a lot like Calcutta. During a rehearsal for the Mass, a Vatican monsignor told me not to look up during the reading "so as not to detract from the transmission of the word of God to the people." But when I got to the podium, I glanced down at the reading from the Book of Wisdom, and then looked out—just for a moment—at the vast throng baking beneath the merciless sun. I steeled myself to keep from choking up.

The echo of my first words through Bernini's columns reminded me to slow down. The pope was seated right behind me. It was an extraordinary moment. Yet, as I returned to my seat, it was impossible not to think of ordinary moments with Mother. I remembered her riding next to me in my red 1982 Honda Prelude, sitting across from me on a flight to San Diego eating Kentucky Fried Chicken, praying intently on her knees in the motherhouse chapel, rubbing the chest of a man dying of AIDS in Gift of Peace.

There was a huge portrait of Mother hanging directly above where Pope Francis was seated. It portrayed her with a halo for she had now joined the company of the elect, the people she venerated throughout her lifetime—Mary, Joseph, Peter, and Paul; her namesake Thérèse of Lisieux; and all the other saints. The irony of this struck me because Mother never thought of herself as special or worthy of praise. She was a handmaid, a servant, or as she put it in her inimitable way, "a pencil in the hand of a loving God." She saw herself like the "useless servant" in the Gospel who did no more than what was her obligation. Mother's duty was the pursuit of holiness. "Holiness is not the privilege of a few but the responsibility of each one of us," she told me repeatedly. She did her duty, as did many before her and many continue to do. The procession of the saints is not limited to the canonized.

Many women now at rest had marched with Mother along the same path of holiness and had reached the same glory. Her sisters, too, had done what was asked of them, and most certainly now enjoyed "the kingdom prepared from the creation of the world." It did not matter that they received no public acclaim or ceremony in Rome—God knew their lives and surely judged them worthy.

Father Celeste Van Exem could legitimately have claimed

to be the cofounder of the Missionaries of Charity and was Mother's closest spiritual advisor. He is buried in a vault in a Calcutta cemetery a few miles from the motherhouse. His resting place is overgrown with weeds and nearly impossible to find. If you do find it, you'll see his name engraved on a wall, the last of nine Jesuits so listed and interred there. His home in eternity was assured and that is all that matters.

Mother knew her life was not about her. She called what she did a "drop in the ocean," and she believed it, too. But she knew her insignificance served as an instrument for God's greatness. Her bearings were simple: She came from God and journeyed home to God. She was just one in the mysterious procession of people throughout time and across cultures who trod the trail toward holiness, doing small things with great love.

For me in the thirty-seven years since I met her—what I refer to as life "after Mother"—the path to holiness has meant imitating her. She is my compass. She often asked me to pray that she didn't "spoil God's work," and I pray each day I don't squander God's gift of Mother to me. I build into my daily routines little reminders of the woman I was lucky enough to befriend. I try to wear something blue every day, just as she did. I hold my rosary in my hand while in church, and walk with urgency when working, just as she did. Each night I read the Gospel for the next day's Mass, just as she did, and each morning recite the same prayer she prayed on waking.

Jesus, through the most pure heart of Mary,
I offer you the prayers, works, joys and sufferings of
this day

For all the intentions of your Divine Heart
In union with all the Masses being offered
throughout the Catholic world.
I offer you my heart.
Make it meek and humble like yours.

Mother was fond of reminding her friends, "If you are too busy to pray, you are too busy." (She said this often; I ignored it too often.) In my office and home, I have photos of her everywhere. Our family prayers always end, "Mother Teresa of Calcutta, pray for us." Mother told Mary and me to be holy and make our home another Nazareth. As a wedding gift, she gave us a framed religious icon with an inscription saying, "Always pray together and you will stay together." Mary and I have done this, and our thirty years of marriage are our living testimony to the woman who has been our lodestar.

I am no saint. I will never be as good or kind as Mother Teresa was no matter how hard I try. But I also know that I can be better than I am, more prayerful, less selfish, more humble, less worldly, more in love with God and less with myself. While I was in her company, I was the very best I could be. I saw the good I was capable of living, as if her holiness rubbed off on me a little. She has been gone for a quarter of a century, and I still feel orphaned.

At times, I find myself like the man in the Gospel who, when seeking a cure for his sick son, was reminded by Jesus that everything is possible to one who trusts; the man cried, "I do believe; help my unbelief!" In such moments, I think of Mother and all she taught me. I am growing in trust, thank

God, while I try to live as strenuously as she did. She told her sisters to give until it hurts and love until it hurts. This is what I strive for. I try to do the extra thing—take on extra chores, be available at all hours for the kids, say yes anytime the MCs ask me to do something, and do hands-on work for people in need whenever I can. I want to be exhausted when I go to bed.

I find much solace in the realization that somehow—mostly due to the good influences of my wife and family, of my friends and spiritual mentors and even enemies—I have become a better person, a better Christian, a better version of myself. I am a giver, not a gatherer. With the help of Mother Teresa's example on earth and her prayers from heaven, I can remain a giver. But there is still a great deal of work to be done.

The Work Goes On

Yesterday is gone. Tomorrow has not come. We have
only today. Let us begin.

—*Mother Teresa*

On a chilly October day, seventy-five sisters of the Mis
sionaries of Charity filed into Old Saint Patrick's
Church in Lower Manhattan for the noon Mass. They were
accompanied by a number of elderly indigent women from
the MC group home a few miles away, as well as by longtime
MC volunteers and other Catholic faithful. We had all come
to celebrate the fiftieth anniversary of the opening of Mother
Teresa's first mission in the United States in 1971.

The church was barely half-full, and there were no representatives from the city or the Catholic hierarchy on hand—a
dramatic contrast to the days when Mother Teresa attended
such Masses and the crowds spilled out of the church sanc-
tuaries, cardinals and bishops presided over the liturgies, and
the media strained to catch any glimpse of her. But the lack
of fanfare added to the intimacy of the occasion. As Mother

taught us, the MCs' work was "for the glory of God and the good of his people," not for the esteem of the worldly.

Sandy McMurtrie, Mary, and I had taken a morning train from Washington to attend the golden jubilee. As Mass began, the voices of the sisters from the choir loft reminded me of the angelic ones I had heard at my first Mass in Calcutta long ago. At the conclusion of the service, the sisters processed up the center aisle, two by two, each carrying a solitary flower that she placed in one of two vases. By the time the procession was complete, the individual flowers of the nuns formed two magnificent floral displays, like little acts of love coming together over time to form something beautiful for God.

The reception in the courtyard that followed felt like a family reunion. I saw Sister Manorama, the first MC I met in Washington in 1985. She was seventy years old, having served everywhere from Sanaa in Yemen to New Bedford, Massachusetts, where she helps run an MC shelter for women and children. Sister Tanya, Mother Teresa's companion for her meetings with Princess Diana, came for the festivities even though she was still recovering from a stay in intensive care due to Covid. I also visited with Sister Maria Chandra, a Hindu convert I hadn't seen since the days we welcomed the first AIDS patients to the Gift of Peace together. These old friends milled about with the younger sisters who'd never had the chance to meet Mother Teresa but nonetheless felt called by God to follow in her footsteps.

The sisters knew well that they could not have done all they had done for America's poorest these last five decades without the volunteers. Helpers like Gene Principe, the man who taught me to care for the dying and who, in his nineties, still works six days a week in the MC's Harlem soup kitchen. Or Michael Aldeguer, who for twenty-two years has lived in a tiny second-floor room in the Gift of Peace, caring full-time for the dying and destitute down the hall. It was moving to see such humble and holy men again. Both are proud to be part of a network of MC volunteers that extends throughout the world. Just as much as the sisters, they continue the work that Mother Teresa set in motion. They, too, serve Jesus "in His distressing disguise of the poorest of the poor."

In the twenty-five years since Mother's death, the Missionaries of Charity have increased in size to become the seventh-largest institute of nuns in the world, with more than 5,100 women and 760 houses in 139 countries. This expansion of the MCs is all the more remarkable considering the 25 percent global decline in vocations to the religious life over the last quarter century. In the United States during that period, the total number of nuns has plummeted by more than half. While the MCs have stayed steady, they face many challenges as new vocations slow to a crawl and a much larger cohort of sisters ages. Mother taught her sisters to take it all in stride, trusting that God sees their needs and will provide.

The work goes on no matter the difficulty or danger. A year after Mother died, three MC sisters were gunned down just outside their convent in the coastal city of Hodeidah, Yemen, by an Islamic extremist convinced he would go to heaven for his deed. Undeterred, the MCs buried their dead and brought in three brave sisters to continue the work with the city's disabled they had started twenty-five years earlier.

Anti-Christian sentiment in Yemen has only intensified in the twenty-first century, especially in Aden, where five MC sisters ran a home for the disabled and elderly. In December 2015, the last Catholic church in the city was burned to the ground. Sister Prema gave each sister the option of being reassigned elsewhere. Abandoning the men and women entrusted to their care, however, was unthinkable for the sisters in Aden.

On the morning of March 4, 2016, the five sisters followed their usual routine: They attended Mass, ate breakfast, put on their aprons, and said the MC's morning prayer:

Let us preach You without preaching,
Not by words, but by our example,
By the catching force,
The sympathetic influence of what we do,
The evident fullness of the love our hearts bear to You.

They then dispersed into the wards to feed and clean the eighty people in their care.

Two men came to the MCs' gate under the pretense of visiting their elderly mother. Once inside, they pulled out automatic weapons and opened fire, killing the security guard who had admitted them and the workers in the courtyard. The pair had come for the five sisters in the name of the Islamic State. They tracked down four of them, bound their hands, and summarily executed them. In the convent chapel, they found Father Tom Uzhunnalil, a missionary priest who had served in Yemen for fourteen years. They smashed the tabernacle and all the statues and religious icons there, and they kidnapped Father Tom. (He would be released un-harmed after eighteen months in captivity.)

The last remaining nun, Sister Sally, had heard the screams and gunshots. She first tried to get to the chapel to warn Father Tom, but when she realized she was too late, she hid herself in a storage room next to the refrigerator, standing motionless behind its open door. Three times, the two gunmen came into the room where she stood in plain view. Each time, they somehow did not see her. After ninety minutes, the men fled the compound, carrying away Father Tom, and leaving behind Sister Sally, the eighty patients, and sixteen dead. After taking time to recover from her traumatic experience, Sister Sally returned to the Middle East, where she continues to serve the poor. The MCs have not yet re-turned to Aden, though they maintain homes elsewhere in Yemen.

Harrowing situations like this go with the territory the MCs occupy, whether it be gang-controlled ghettoes in the United States or Arabian cities ravaged by civil war. When the government in Afghanistan collapsed in 2021 with the U.S. military withdrawal, the five sisters operating an MC home for severely handicapped children in Kabul were faced with a choice. There was a plane leaving for Italy with five seats for them. But the sisters refused to leave the eleven girls and three boys in their home and preferred to remain at the mercy of the Taliban. By God's grace and the help of the Italian government, the sisters and all fourteen disabled children were spirited from the country on the second-to-last plane out before the city fell. (They now live in a group home just outside Rome.)

The MCs in India faced an equally deadly challenge last year, as the subcontinent became the epicenter of the Covid pandemic, with a death toll numbering in the millions. By the end of 2021, fifty-nine sisters had died from the virus, including the superiors of seven homes. This tragedy did not deter the others from doing all the government permitted them to do to alleviate the misery of those suffering from the virus and the economic catastrophe it inflicted.

The work is far less perilous in many places, but it is just as hard. In Miami, the sisters feed hundreds each day at their soup kitchen, and the twenty-five beds in their women's shelter are always filled. In Baltimore, the MCs run a home for women, visit the imprisoned, and bring cheer to elderly shut-ins. A new home specializing in indigent tuberculosis patients opened in Rosarito, Mexico, in 2021. Around the world, the sisters adapt their services to offer what is most needed, but the daily routine Mother established continues unchanged. They get up at 4:40 a.m., wash their clothes by hand, adhere to a strict schedule of prayer, and look forward to being together in the convent for meals and evening recreation. Working with the poorest of the poor remains their mission and duty.

It took me years to understand what Mother meant when she said that Calcutta was everywhere if you only had eyes to see. The destitution I witnessed on my 1985 trip can be found in other forms in superficially affluent countries plagued by teenage suicide, drug use, the isolation of the elderly, and what Pope John Paul II termed "the culture of death" that surrounds abortion and euthanasia. Spiritual and material poverty are two sides of the same coin.

"Do we know who our own poor are?" Mother asked a gathering of bishops in Rome in 1980.

Do we know our neighbor, the poor of our own area? It is so easy for us to talk and talk about the poor of other places. Very often we have the suffering, we have the lonely, we have the people—old, unwanted, feeling miserable—and they are near us and we don't even know them. We have no time even to smile at them. Tuberculosis and cancer [are] not the great diseases. I think a much greater disease is to be unwanted, unloved. The pain that these people suffer is very difficult to understand, to penetrate. I think this is what our people all over the world are going through, in every family, in every home. This suffering is being repeated in every man, woman and child. I think Christ is undergoing his Passion again. And it is for you and for me to help them.

At our last meeting, ten weeks before she died, I thanked Mother for introducing me to Jesus in the person of the poor and teaching me to strive for a life that is other-minded. It took her mentorship and hands-on work for me to realize that the poor, too, are often very powerful people. They possess the power to unleash compassion from within us and transform our lives if we let them. They protect and preserve what is truly human in each of us. They have the power to form caring communities all over the world, just like the one that gathered that October afternoon in 2021 at Manhattan's Old Saint Pat's.

Humans are today increasingly distant from one another, and rapid advances in technology and artificial intelligence are accelerating this dehumanization. Mother said, "The poor are the hope and salvation of mankind." These people who thirst for companionship and seek our time and care provide us a path toward meaningful, purposeful lives. Anyone stretched by the needs of another, such as a husband caring for a wife with a chronic or terminal illness, or a foster mom nurturing an abused child, knows the liberating joy of good deeds done for love, especially ones that cost us. Scripture says it is more blessed to give than to receive, and Mother said we must "give until it hurts."

Those who feed the hungry, clothe the naked, visit the sick or imprisoned, welcome the stranger, or comfort the lonely know that their efforts may be but a temporary respite. We aren't likely to change the world as Mother did, but we can change the world of those around us, starting in our own families and neighborhoods, bringing a smile to the forlorn, hope to the despairing, and love to the unloved. The vast ocean is made up of little drops.

Near the end of her life, Mother Teresa was asked about the fact that little seemed to have changed in Calcutta despite her efforts, that for every person she helped die in peace, there still were ten outside dying alone. She said she wasn't discouraged at all. "God doesn't call me to be successful. God calls me to be faithful."

To some, her call to faithfulness is a religious imperative. To others, it is a social pledge to our brothers and sisters in need. To all of us, it is a call to action.

Acknowledgments

These pages describe my debt to Mother Teresa and to the members of her Missionaries of Charity family. It is not possible to name all the individuals of this saintly group of women and men whose exemplary lives have helped shape my own. I must, however, mention Father Joseph Langford, whom Mother chose to start her order of priests. He convinced me to leave my job and live with the MC Fathers for a year, discerned with me that I was not called to the priesthood, and gave me his holy blessing in Mexico City on the day of my engagement to Mary Sarah Griffith. He and my spiritual brothers in Tijuana, and the sisters of the Missionaries of Charity I've come to know all over the world in the past thirty-seven years, hold a special place in my heart. This book hopes to honor their friendship and faithful witness to the joy of the Gospel.

My family has been exceptionally supportive throughout the project, beginning with Mary, my glorious wife of thirty years. Her love, encouragement, feedback, and superb suggestions have been invaluable. Our children—Jamie (and his wife, Carolyn, and their sons, Sebastian and Patrick), Joe, Max, John, and Marie—are the primary reason I wrote this book. I wanted them to meet the Mother Teresa that their parents knew. My own mother, Florence; my twin sister, Jeannine, and her husband, Bruce Hubbard; and my older siblings Ed, Patrice, and Maureen, met Mother during her lifetime. Memories of those encounters continue to gladden and unite us as a family.

This book would not have been possible without my friend Dan D'Aniello. Dan provided me the benefit of his wisdom over the last decade and supported my professional efforts and this book at every turn. He is a humble man of God who privately and faithfully helps many pursue their dreams and live their Christian vocations. His life as a Catholic layman, loving husband and father, servant of the country he cherishes, and leader in the business world inspires me and all those privileged to know him.

Sandy McMurtrie was Mother Teresa's close friend and later mine. She vouched for me when I first began my work for the MCs in the mid-1980s. It was a Himalayan challenge for an unmarried man to earn the trust of Mother and her sisters. Sandy accelerated that process by including me in the tight circle that surrounded and supported Mother during her stays in the United States and when she was hospitalized in Calcutta. Sandy and her children are blessings to me. Her youngest daughter, Maria Guadalupe, was adopted from Mother Teresa's orphanage in Mexico City. Having Mother as her godmother made my job as Maria Guadalupe's godfather easy!

There are four others who facilitated my early encounters with Mother: Ralph Dyer, Jan Petrie, and Sunita and Naresh Kumar. Ralph left this world in 2003, and I am grateful for his and their friendship every day. In addition, Dan and Kathy Mezzalingua, Brian Olson, Jan Sterns, John and Therese Casey and their children, Bridget Leonard, Tim and Nancy Joyce, Teresa Cotter, Bernadette Rienzo, Cathy and Mike Nagle, Tish Holmes, Shep Abell, Michael and Laura Timmis, and Fathers Stanislaus Wadowski, Gilles Hetier and Paul Scalia became some of my dearest friends through our mutual admiration of or work for Mother.

The idea of writing this book came from a conversation more than twenty years ago with Mother's successor as superior general of the MCs, Sister Nirmala. She gave me her blessing on the project, as did her successor, Sister Prema. The demands of raising five children and my many professional responsibilities in the intervening years kept me from pursuing my plan. When my term as president of Ave Maria University ended in 2020 and the Covid-19 pandemic began, I finally was able to turn my full attention to the book project. Nothing like lockdowns to free up writing time!

No biography of Mother Teresa can be written without a heavy reliance on three literary sources: *Such a Vision of the Street* by Eileen Egan, *Something Beautiful for God* by Malcolm Muggeridge, and *Come Be My Light* by Brian Kolodiejchuk, MC. These are the starting points for anyone thinking about Mother's life. I further had the benefit of hundreds of pages of notes I took over the years in my many interactions with her and those close to her. My lifelong habit of journaling enabled me to contemporaneously record the words and events recounted in this work.

A first-time author needs plenty of guidance in writing a book, and during the drafting of my original manuscript, my Tallahassee friend Bonnie Woodbery, a professor of English, was invaluable. She devoted untold hours of attention to the initial chapters I wrote. Her critical review, careful edits, and calm reassurance helped me get the document to the point where I could consider shopping it to a publisher. Others, too, provided valuable feedback and suggestions in the early stages of the project: Kathy Mezzalingua, Sister Nirmala Maria, Kevin Tobin, Terry Boulos, Arthur Brooks, Sister Christie, Chris Donahue, Dave Lawrence, and Sister Ozana. They were always there for me when I needed them, full of wisdom and encouragement. Father Brian Kolodiejchuk was another member of this group and deserves special mention for having read the finished manuscript to check my memories against his knowledge. I could have had no better friend and aid in writing about Mother. My daughter, Marie, took the final draft to Minnesota in January and read it to my beloved twin whose beauty, grace, and sense of humor were not diminished even slightly by the challenges amyotrophic lateral sclerosis (ALS) presented. Jeannine inspired every word of every page of this book.

Considering the fact that I had no literary agent, it is a small miracle that this book found any publisher, much less the gold standard. There were two people responsible for this amazing grace: Mother Teresa and Priscilla Painton, vice president and editorial director of nonfiction at Simon & Schuster. Back in 2010, when Priscilla was a relatively new editor at the house, she graciously met with me as a courtesy to one of her authors (my buddy Karl Rove) and discussed what a book on Mother might look like. Ten years passed before I could follow her advice. I then sent a "Hail Mary" email to her. Not only did she remember me, she graciously asked for a book proposal and sample of what I had written.

Priscilla then passed my proposal to her colleague Robert Messenger, a gentleman and master of the art of writing and storytelling. He pointed out that the twenty-fifth anniversary of Mother Teresa's death in September 2022 presented both a wonderful opportunity and a compressed timeline for publication. To accelerate the rewriting process, Robert suggested I contact a former colleague of his, Emily MacLean, to see if she would be willing to help reorganize my material and streamline its contents. With children ages one and three at home, and dozens of unpacked boxes awaiting her attention from a recent move, Emily had ample grounds to decline, but she didn't. Over the ensuing months, she helped me tell my story in my own words but in a way I never could have done on my own. They brought out the best in my writing and did so with winsome ease. Two finer professionals and people you will not meet. My experiences with Bonnie, Robert, and Emily have awakened me to the transformative power great editors exercise. Every time I open this book, I will remember with gratitude what they did for me.

I could not have undertaken this literary assignment without the full support of the board of directors of Aging with Dignity, the nonprofit where I am happily employed. Guy Smith (chairman and mentor), Zim Boulos (vice-chairman and best friend), Bobby Brochin (first-rate Miami lawyer and even better human being), and Patricia Russell (a lovely and loyal advocate for the elderly and dying) all deserve individual mention. They were there beside me in

1996 when I founded the organization and have played an invaluable role in its becoming a leading voice in support of God-given human dignity and humane care at the end of life. Especial thanks, also, to the dedicated staff in our Tallahassee and Virginia offices who have been an immense help throughout the nearly three years of this book's writing.

Tricia Flatley deserves special mention here. She is a wonderful friend and supporter who for many years urged me to write this book. Her parents were friends and benefactors of Mother Teresa when she opened two houses in their native state of Massachusetts. At the opening of the MCs' New Bedford home in 1995, Tricia met Mother for the first time and shared with her the misfortune that she had no children. "God does not want you to be childless," Mother assured her, and she gave Tricia a Miraculous Medal and instructed her to ask for Our Lady's intercession. Eighteen months (and one miscarriage) later, Tricia gave birth to the twin girls who are the joy of her life. Tricia and her siblings carry on the compassionate philanthropy of their parents— humbly, quietly, and effectively.

My friend Michael Collopy, perhaps the finest portrait photographer of his generation, generously granted me use of the image that adorns the cover of this book, as well as the one from Mother's canonization Mass in Saint Peter's Square. Mother Teresa hated being photographed, yet Michael managed to capture the incredible beauty of his dear friend's life in the book *Works of Love Are Works of Peace: Mother Teresa of Calcutta and the Missionaries of Charity*. He inspires awe. I also am grateful to the others whose photos are displayed in this book with their permission, particularly my friend Prasad of Prasad Photography in Newport Beach, California, another exceptional photographer.

Getting the book to the finish line required hard work by my copy editor Richard Willett. My son John assisted with the proofing and quote checks. Many thanks to them.

Finally, I want to thank the poor, disabled, mentally ill, abandoned elderly, and others in need who have revealed to me their great dignity and my need for relationship with them. Mother Teresa was a bridge for me to these often neglected souls. If this book moves the hearts of its readers to reach out to them with love and compassion, then it will have served its purpose.

Notes

In addition to stories in my own journals, notes, and correspondence, I have included in this book material from a conference that Archabbot Douglas Nowicki, O.S.B., and I convened at Saint Vincent College in Latrobe, Pennsylvania, on October 5–7, 2007, to commemorate the ten-year anniversary of Mother's death. Sister Nirmala, Father Brian Kolodiejchuk, Agi Guttadauro, Sandy McMurtrie, Jan Petrie, Roni Daniels, Dr. Patricia Aubanel, Father Bob Conroy, Arturo Mercado, Bradley James, Brother Sebastian, Michael Collopy, Dr. Larry Kline, and others shared their extraordinary stories at this gathering, and I have included some of that material in this book. Sandy McMurtrie graciously granted me permission to use excerpts of her testimony for the Cause for the Beatification of Mother Teresa. I also have included material from a series of talks Sister Monica gave to the MC Fathers in 1988 in Tijuana, Mexico, as well as conversations with her and Father Joseph Langford.

The notes in this section record the other sources—books, newspapers, magazines, journals, and online publications—from which I gathered content for this book. All Bible references are to the New American Bible, Saint Joseph Edition, 1970, unless noted otherwise.

INTRODUCTION
The Mother I Knew

2   *Their efforts were aided by six*: Susan Caba, "Requiem for a Saint: Funeral for Simple, Pure Mother Teresa Presents a Host of Complexities," *Spokesman-Review*, September 11, 1997, https://www.spokesman.com/stories/1997/sep/11/requiem-for-a-saint-funeral-for-simple-pure/.

4   *"For I was hungry and you gave"*: Matthew 25:35–45 (Jerusalem Bible Reader's Edition (New York: Double-Day, 1968)).

4   *"The work is only the expression"*: Malcolm Muggeridge, *Something Beautiful for God* (New York: HarperCollins, 1971), 98.

CHAPTER 1
Calcutta

9   *During her first decade in the city*: Office of the Registrar General & Census Commissioner, India, "A-2 Decadal Variation In Population Since 1901: West Bengal," censusindia.gov.in/2011census/PCA/A2_Data_Table.html.

11   *"For those of us who find difficulty"*: Muggeridge, *Something Beautiful*, 126.

12   *"Sinners lick the earth, that is"*: Blaise Pascal, *Oeuvres Completes* (Paris: Seuil, 1963), 602.

14   *"to go out and give the life of Christ"*: Eileen Egan, *Such a Vision of the Street* (New York: Doubleday, 1985), 12.

14   *Gonxha had grown up ethnic Albanian*: Ibid., 6.

14   *Her mother, Drana, was a deeply*: Ibid., 7–8.

14   *She never turned away the needy*: Ibid., 8.

14   *Nikola was a successful merchant*: Ibid., 6.

14   *In 1919, he traveled to a dinner*: Ibid., 8–9.

15 *When he returned home gravely ill*: Kathryn Spink, *Mother Teresa: A Complete Authorized Biography* (New York: HarperCollins, 1997), 6.

15 *The priest arrived in the Bojaxhiu home*: Egan, *Such a Vision*, 8–9.

15 *Immediately following Nikola's death*: Spink, *Mother Teresa*, 6.

15 *It was only Drana's fortitude*: Egan, *Such a Vision*, 9.

15 *"Put your hand in Jesus' hand"*: Brian Kolodiejchuk, *Mother Teresa: Come Be My Light* (New York: Doubleday, 2007), 13.

15 *Gonxha wept as the train pulled away*: Egan, *Such a Vision*, 14; Kerry Walters, *St. Teresa of Calcutta: Missionary, Mother, Mystic* (Cincinnati: Franciscan Media, 2016), 9.

16 *Gonxha stayed in Ireland studying English*: Spink, *Mother Teresa*, 12.

16 *"Fine and pure as summer dew"*: Kolodiejchuk, *Mother Teresa*, 15–17.

16 *She spent Christmas without a Mass*: Egan, *Such a Vision*, 15; Walters, *St. Teresa of Calcutta*, 10.

16 *"Many families live in the streets"*: Spink, *Mother Teresa*, 13–14.

17 *She reached Calcutta on January 6*: Kolodiejchuk, *Mother Teresa*, 17.

17 *In a letter she sent home*: Ibid.

18 *"The heat of India is simply burning"*: Ibid., 18–19.

19 *"a drop in the ocean"*: Muggeridge, 119.

CHAPTER 2

Meeting Mother

30 *In 1931, the newly professed*: Egan, *Such a Vision*, 19.

30 *Sister Teresa taught history and*: Walters, *St. Teresa of Calcutta*, 17; Egan, *Such a Vision*, 22.

30   *In May 1937, Sister Teresa took*: Kolodiejchuk, *Mother Teresa*, 23.

31   *"Every Sunday I visit the poor"*: Ibid., 27.

31   *Saint Mary's School had been requisitioned*: Ibid., 35–36.

31   *She was taking care of three hundred*: Ibid., 36–37.

32   *She was ordered to take hours*: Egan, *Such a Vision*, 27; Kolodiejchuk, *Mother Teresa*, 36–37.

32   *It would become known as*: Egan, *Such a Vision*, 24.

32   *Mother Teresa and her hundreds*: Kolodiejchuk, *Mother Teresa*, 37.

33   *Because she had no food*: Egan, *Such a Vision*, 24.

33   *"We were not supposed to go out"*: Ibid.

CHAPTER 3

To Choose Always the Hardest

41   *While in prayer she heard*: John 19:28.

41   *" 'I thirst' is something much deeper"*: Joseph Langford, *Mother Teresa's Secret Fire* (Huntington, IN: Our Sunday Visitor, 2008), 56.

41   *"The message was quite clear"*: Egan, *Such a Vision*, 25.

41   *"I am a servant of the Lord"*: Luke 1:38.

42   *"Total surrender and loving trust"*: Mother Teresa, Instructions to MC Sisters, 1983; Joseph Langford, *I Thirst: 40 Days with Mother Teresa* (Greenwood Village, CO: Augustine Institute, 2018), 42.

42   *She described how she saw*: Kolodiejchuk, *Mother Teresa*, 99.

42   *The following month, in January 1948*: Ibid., 102.

43   *"If you were in India"*: Ibid., 106.

43   *It was, she said, "much harder"*: Egan, *Such a Vision*, 31.

43   *So Mother went to Patna*: Ibid., 31, 35.

44   *They gave her practical advice*: Ibid., 34–35.

44   *Mother Teresa returned to Calcutta*: Ibid., 33.

44 *One Calcutta priest said*: Desmond Doig, *Mother Teresa: Her People and Her Work* (New York: Nacheketa, 1976), 53.

44 *Another attributed her works to*: Spink, *Mother Teresa*, 40.

45 *In the slums, she met only*: Kolodiejchuk, *Mother Teresa*, 132.

45 *"old man lying on the street"*: Ibid, 132.

45 *"a very poor woman dying"*: Ibid.

45 *But the poor were happy to have her*: Egan, *Such a Vision*, 37; Muggeridge, *Something Beautiful*, 87.

45 *"Today I learned a good lesson"*: Kolodiejchuk, *Mother Teresa*, 133–34.

46 *She suffered "tortures of loneliness"*: Ibid., 134.

46 *The first young woman to join her*: Egan, *Such a Vision*, 29.

46 *Within a year, Mother Teresa had twelve*: Doig, *Mother Teresa*, 70.

46 *The untold sacrifices of this first cohort*: Egan, *Such a Vision*, 42.

48 *During this time, she receives*: Muggeridge, *Something Beautiful*, 105.

49 *"For the honor and Glory of God"*: Recited by MCs taking final vows at the Basilica of the National Shrine of the Immaculate Conception, Washington, D.C., December 8, 2021, author's records.

50 *"We started our work as the suffering"*: Egan, *Such a Vision*, 14.

50 *"In the choice of works, there was neither"*: Egan, *Such a Vision*, 44.

50 *"Jesus went about doing good"*: Acts 10:38.

CHAPTER 4
Spiritual Poverty

55 *"there is no hunger for bread"*: Doig, *Mother Teresa*, 159.

56 *"I took her to the hospital"*: Muggeridge, *Something Beautiful*, 91.

57 *A Muslim health officer offered*: Spink, *Mother Teresa*, 54; Doig, *Mother Teresa*, 59.

57 *She named it Nirmal Hriday*: Doig, *Mother Teresa*, 59.

57 *"wholehearted and free service to"*: From the Constitution of the Missionaries of Charity.

57 *Opposition to Mother at Kalighat*: Doig, *Mother Teresa*, 87; Egan, *Such a Vision*, 67.

57 *She kept meticulous handwritten records*: Doig, *Mother Teresa*, 138.

58 *"We help them to die with God"*: Ibid.

58 *Mother was careful to observe*: Ibid., 147.

58 *"I have lived like an animal"*: Egan, *Such a Vision*, 49.

59 *Mother opened a health clinic*: Ibid., 75.

59 *She operated mobile leprosy clinics*: Ibid., 81.

59 *In 1961, she began plans*: Ibid., 139.

59 *"The conditions under which the leper"*: Kolodiejchuk, *Mother Teresa*, 175–76.

60 *By 1975, more than one thousand sisters were stationed*: Ibid, 267.

61 *The most meaningful recognition*: Edward Le Joly S.J., *Mother Teresa: A Woman in Love* (Notre Dame, IN: Ave Maria, 1993), 56.

61 *He brought a plate of food*: Ibid., 53, 55.

61 *"Nirmal Hriday proclaims the profound dignity"*: Mary Farrow, "The Happiest Day of Mother Teresa's Life," *Catholic News Agency*, December 22, 2016, www.catholic newsagency.com/amp/news/34441/the-happiest-day -of-mother-teresas-life (accessed January 3, 2022).

61 *"our poor people are great people"*: Mother Teresa, "Nobel Acceptance Speech," Oslo, Norway, December 10, 1979, accessed January 3, 2021, https://www.nobelprize.org /prizes/peace/1979/teresa/acceptance-speech/.

62 *"People today are hungry for love"*: Doig, *Mother Teresa*, 159.

62 *"When I pick up a person"*: "Nobel Acceptance Speech."

CHAPTER 5
A Born Entrepreneur

67 *"a kindness in her gaze"*: Langford, *Secret Fire*, 37.

67 *"a new hope in what was best"*: Langford, *Secret Fire*, 38.

68 *In the early years, for example*: Muggeridge, *Something Beautiful*, 102.

68 *Eileen Egan, a staff member*: Egan, *Such a Vision*, 45.

73 *The figure was draped in*: Susan DeFord, "A Revered Memory That's Not for Sale: Guardians of Mother Teresa's Legacy Resist Efforts to Cash In on Her Name for Good Causes or Greedy Purposes," *Washington Post*, December 20, 1997, B9.

CHAPTER 6
A Calling

79 *"Without Our Lady we cannot stand"*: Kolodiejchuk, *Mother Teresa*, 141.

80 *"My Sisters, Father, are the gift"*: Ibid., 212.

80 *She believed that if the pregnant*: Luke 1:39.

82 *Mother remained by her side*: Egan, *Such a Vision*, 140.

82 *Mother called Agnes*: Le Joly, *Mother Teresa*, 25.

82 *When she finally received word*: Kolodiejchuk, *Mother Teresa*, 173.

83 *Her mother wrote to her*: Egan, *Such a Vision*, 151.

83 *In 1965, she went to the Albanian*: Ibid., 151–54.

83 *She said to the Albanian official*: Ibid., 153.

83 *"You don't know what this sacrifice"*: Ibid., 387.

83 *Mother Teresa received word in July*: Spink, *Mother Teresa*, 97.

87 *a place Mother Teresa described*: Mother Teresa, General Letter to the Missionaries of Charity, July 23, 1989.

CHAPTER 7
Mother of Outcasts

96 *Mother Teresa's earliest forays into*: Egan, *Such a Vision*, 79.

97 *By the time I came to witness*: Spink, *Mother Teresa*, 203.

97 *The Gospels record his healing of lepers*: Matthew 8:1–4; Luke 17:11–15.

97 *his tenderness toward the Samaritan woman*: John 4:4–42.

97 *and the adulteress thrown at his feet*: John 8:1–11.

97 *the parable of the Good Samaritan*: Luke 10:25–37.

97 *Jesus said, "Come to me"*: Matthew 11:28.

CHAPTER 8
A Human Heart

107 *"Holiness does not make you less human"*: Pope Francis, *Gaudete et Exsultate* [Apostolic Exhortation on the Call to Holiness in Today's World], sec. 34, accessed January 3, 2022, https://www.vatican.va/content/francesco /en/apost_exhortations/documents/papa-francesco_esort azione-ap_20180319_gaudete-et-exsultate.html.

110 *She spoke five languages fluently*: Egan, *Such a Vision*, 153.

110 *She once told a friend*: Ibid., 366.

111 *"Any country that accepts abortion"*: Mother Teresa, "Speech at National Prayer Breakfast" (Washington, D.C., February 5, 1994), *Catholic News Agency*, accessed January 3, 2022, https://www.catholicnewsagency.com /resource/55399/blessed-mother-teresa-on-abortion.

113 *"Meetings have a terrible sickening effect"*: Kolodiejchuk, *Mother Teresa*, 223.

113 *"Sometimes I have been rather quick"*: Ibid., 171.

113 *In April 1942, she made*: Ibid., 28.

114 *a broken leg*: Doig, *Mother Teresa*, 90.

114 *a broken shoulder, and three*: Kolodiejchuk, *Mother Teresa*, 324.

114 *a compound fracture of her left*: Egan, *Such a Vision*, 161.

114 *nineteen stitches in her head*: Ibid., 414.

114 *two stitches after being bitten*: Spink, *Mother Teresa*, 276.

114 *Mother quietly suffered dozens of bouts*: Egan, *Such a Vision*, 287.

114 *tuberculosis*: Doig, *Mother Teresa*, 61.

114 *five heart attacks*: Rome, 1983; Tijuana, 1989; and Calcutta in 1993, 1996, and 1997.

114 *a stroke*: Spink, *Mother Teresa*, 182.

114 *and two pacemaker surgeries*: Le Joly, *Mother Teresa*, 181.

114 *She had deformed, misshapen feet*: Spink, *Mother Teresa*, 18.

114 *She believed "suffering can become"*: Muggeridge, *Something Beautiful*, 108.

118 *"We are so different," Mother Teresa commented*: Spink, *Mother Teresa*, 107.

119 *"She gave me total freedom"*: Ibid., 112.

119 *"Be kind to each other"*: Kolodiejchuk, *Mother Teresa*, 196.

119 *Pope Francis, although he met her*: CBS News, "Pope Francis Sets Day to Make Mother Teresa a Saint," March 15, 2016, accessed January 4, 2022, https://www.cbsnews.com/news/pope-francis-canonization-mother-teresa-september-4/.

119 *On that occasion he called her*: Holy See Press Office, "Mother Teresa of Calcutta, Tireless Worker of Mercy,"

September 4, 2016, accessed January 4, 2022, https://press.vatican.va/content/salastampa/en/bollettino/pubblico/2016/09/04/160904a.html.

120 *"Mercy," she said, "had become second nature"*: Edward Pentin, "Mother Teresa Saw Jesus in Everyone," *National Catholic Register*, August 30, 2016, accessed January 4, 2022, https://www.ncregister.com/news/mother-teresa-saw-jesus-in-everyone.

CHAPTER 9

A Joyful Christian

124 *Saint Paul wrote, "Rejoice with those"*: Romans 12:15–16.
124 *When a friend told Mother*: Egan, *Such a Vision*, 315.
124 *At a border checkpoint crossing*: Ibid., 412.
125 *In the car between events*: Ibid., 208.
130 *"They told me about the violence"*: Ibid., 174.

CHAPTER 10

In the Palace

135 *She described a 1976 visit to Philadelphia*: Kolodiejchuk, *Mother Teresa*, 278.
136 *"This celebrity has been forced on me"*: Egan, *Such a Vision*, 365.
137 *"She had embodied many of"*: George Weigel, *Witness to Hope: The Biography of Pope John Paul II* (New York: HarperCollins, 1999), 818.
137 *A year later when he returned*: Egan, *Such a Vision*, 339.
137 *"The Pope visited India to lift up"*: George Weigel, *The End and the Beginning: Pope John Paul II—The Victory of Freedom, the Last Years, the Legacy* (New York: Doubleday, 2010), 18.

137 *Soon after John Paul's return from that trip*: Weigel, *Witness to Hope*, 566.

138 *Tennyson wrote, "We needs must love"*: Alfred, Lord Tennyson, *Idylls of the King* (London: Penguin, 2004).

138 *Actress Penelope Cruz spent a week in Calcutta*: Hilary De Vries, "Penelope Cruz: Will She Say I Do, or I Don't," *Marie Claire*, January 9, 2009, accessed January 4, 2022, https://www.marieclaire.com/celebrity/a156/penelope-cruz/.

138 *and reported after their meeting*: Brut Media, "The Life of Penelope Cruz," February 1, 2020, accessed January 4, 2022, https://www.brut.media/us/entertainment/the-life-of-penelope-cruz-040ef88b-5ac9-44d5-be09-bbd076bb60d8.

139 *"To meet her is to feel utterly humble"*: Egan, *Such a Vision*, 357.

139 *Mother praised the prime minister*: Ibid., 198.

139 *In 1984, Indira Gandhi was assassinated*: Ibid., 402.

139 *At the funeral, Mother Teresa prayed*: Ibid.

140 *Mother Teresa told her friend*: Ibid., 66.

140 *In 1979, she wrote to Jimmy Carter*: Mother Teresa to President Jimmy Carter, November 17, 1979, in *Forest Park Review*, accessed January 4, 2022, https://www.forestparkreview.com/2006/01/17/mother-teresas-letter-to-president-carter/.

140 *Mother told him that all he*: Egan, *Such a Vision*, 391.

140 *Asked by reporters later*: Ibid.

140 *"The presence of nuclear"*: Ibid., 392.

141 *When Mother Teresa was hospitalized*: Spink, *Mother Teresa*, 191.

141 *In June that year, the president*: Le Joly, *Mother Teresa*, 136.

141   *After presenting the medal to her*: Ibid., 137.

143   *"As per our conversation regarding saving unborn children"*: Mother Teresa to President Bill and Hillary Clinton, Calcutta, February 5, 1994, author's records.

143   *"I often pray for you both"*: Mother Teresa to Hillary Clinton, New York, February 7, 1994, author's records.

143   *"It was February 1994, and she had just delivered a speech"*: Hillary Clinton, "Let's Make Adoptions Easier," Talking It Over, *The Washington Post*, July 30, 1995.

146   *Diana wrote later that day*: Jessica Rach, "Paul Burrell Shares Unseen Letter Princess Diana Wrote After Visiting Mother Teresa's Calcutta Convent in 1992 Revealing She Had 'Found the Direction' She'd Been 'Searching for All These Years,'" *Daily Mail*, May 11, 2020, accessed January 4, 2022, https://www.dailymail.co.uk/femail/article-8306801/Paul-Burrell-shares-unseen-note-Princess-Diana-wrote-him.html.

148   *In Barak's description, she "ended up holding hands"*: Daphne Barak, "Mother Teresa," *Ladies' Home Journal*, April 1996, 146.

149   *On that day, the princess met*: Kate Watson-Smyth, "A Bronx Tale: Hugs and Kisses for Diana and Mother Teresa," *Independent*, June 18, 1997, accessed January 4, 2022, https://www.independent.co.uk/news/a-bronx-tale-hugs-and-kisses-for-diana-and-mother-teresa-1256668.html.

149   *Shortly after the visit, Princess Diana*: Jennifer Calfas, "See the 5 Dresses That Helped Princess Diana Raise Millions for Charity Before She Died," *Money*, August 31, 2017, accessed January 4, 2022, https://money.com/princess-diana-dresses-charity-death/.

149 *Mother Teresa's last public statement*: Associated Press, "Nun and Princess Bound by Altruism," *Seattle Times*, September 6, 1997, accessed January 4, 2022, https://archive.seattletimes.com/archive/?date=19970906&slug =2558750.

150 *Before the princess was laid to rest*: Rebecca Flood, "Princess Diana Found Her 'Calling' Following Spiritual Meeting with Mother Teresa," *Express*, August 21, 2017, accessed January 4, 2022, https://www.express.co.uk /news/world/844100/Princess-Diana-mother-Teresa -spiritual-calling-meeting-Paul-Burrell.

CHAPTER 11
Answering the Critics

151 *"Mother Teresa offered them no option"*: Spink, *Mother Teresa*, 253.

152 *He liked to draw attention*: Matt Cherry interview, "Hitchens on Mother Teresa," *Free Inquiry*, Fall 1996.

153 *"a political operative . . . an accomplice"*: Christopher Hitchens, *The Missionary Position* (London: Verso, 1995), 11.

154 *If He did not condemn a woman*: John 8:1–11.

157 *"The care facilities are grotesquely simple"*: Cherry interview with Hitchens.

158 *"We all have a duty to serve God"*: Spink, *Mother Teresa*, 247.

159 *"Under the cloak of avowed poverty"*: Cherry interview with Hitchens.

160 *"The vast sums of money"*: Christopher Hitchens, "The Devil and Mother Teresa," *Vanity Fair*, October 2001.

161 *Germaine Greer once shared the same cabin*: Germaine Greer, "Unmasking the Mother," *Newsweek*, September 22, 1997, 33.

163 *Perhaps the most offensive of the criticisms*: Bruno Maddox, "Books in Brief: Nonfiction," *New York Times*, January 14, 1996, accessed January 4, 2022, https://www.nytimes.com/1996/01/14/books/books-in-brief-nonfiction-068195.html.

163 *How Hitchens could visit Kalighat*: Christopher Hitchens, "Mother Teresa (Agnes Bojaxhiu)," in *The Quotable Hitchens: from Alcohol to Zionism*, ed. Windsor Mann (Cambridge: Da Capo, 2011), 194.

164 *"I love all religions, but I am"*: Mother Teresa in *The Joy in Loving: A Guide to Daily Living*, ed. Jaya Chalika and Edward Le Joly (New York: Penguin, 1996), 158.

164 *"There is only one God and He"*: Mother Teresa in *A Simple Path*, ed. Lucinda Vardey (New York: Ballantine, 1995), 31.

165 *Hitchens called her "a sly and worldly"*: Hitchens, "The Devil and Mother Teresa."

165 *"my day of vindication may come"*: Ibid.

165 *In 2021, Michelle Goldberg*: Michelle Goldberg, "Was Mother Teresa a Cult Leader?" *New York Times*, May 21, 2021, accessed January 4, 2022, https://www.nytimes.com/2021/05/21/opinion/mother-teresa.html.

CHAPTER 12
In Darkness as in Light

169 *Jesus said, "Whoever wishes to be"*: Luke 9:23.

170 *"She gave me the papers"*: Kolodiejchuk, *Mother Teresa*, 209.

170 *"Please pray specially for me"*: Ibid., 149.

170 *Except for a five-week*: Ibid., 177.

171 *"Lord, my God, who am"*: Ibid., 187.

171 *"Thoughts put on paper give"*: Ibid., 186.

171 *"In my soul," Mother wrote*: Ibid., 193.

171   *"In the call You said that"*: Ibid.

171   *"Souls hold no attraction—Heaven"*: Ibid., 169.

172   *"People say they are drawn closer"*: Ibid., 238.

173   *As Saint Paul wrote of his*: Colossians 1:24.

173   *The Gospel of Mark's account*: Mark 15:33–34.

173   *"In my heart there is no faith"*: Kolodiejchuk, *Mother Teresa*, 193.

174   *In a 1961 letter*: Ibid., 214.

174   *Toward the end of her life*: Ibid., 326.

174   *In 1962, she wrote, "The physical situation"*: Ibid., 232.

174   *"Instead of stifling her missionary impulse"*: Ibid., 185.

175   *As Father Brian wrote, "At prayer"*: Ibid., 212.

175   *"a delicate gift of God"*: Ibid., 6.

175   *"when you make it public"*: Ibid., 327.

175   *Indeed, she wanted to keep*: Ibid., 199.

175   *"the deep things of God"*: 1 Corinthians 2:10.

176   *"Please do not give anything"*: Kolodiejchuk, *Mother Teresa*, 5.

176   *She begged Father Picachy*: Ibid., 199.

176   *Mother succeeded in hiding her secret*: Ibid., 176.

176   *"The whole time smiling"*: Ibid., 187.

177   *In his book* Mother Teresa's Secret Fire: Langford, *Mother Teresa's*, 31.

177   *She once explained, "Cheerfulness is"*: Kolodiejchuk, *Mother Teresa*, 33.

178   *"This year has been a gift of God"*: Mother Teresa, General Letter to Missionaries of Charity Co-Workers, Christmas 1996.

178   *A woman once brought her very sick*: Egan, *Such a Vision*, 257.

178 *"It often happens that those"*: Kolodiejchuk, *Mother Teresa*, 248.

178 *"If I ever become a Saint"*: Ibid., 230.

CHAPTER 13
Saying Goodbye

183 *To promote my new endeavor, Mother wrote*: Mother Teresa, Open Letter to the People of Florida, August 7, 1996.

184 *On November 22, she suffered*: Andrew Gumbel, "Mother Teresa Pleads with Her Friends: Just Let Me Die," *Independent*, December 2, 1996.

184 *Doctors there reprogrammed her pacemaker*: Associated Press, "'Cheerful' Mother Teresa Remains in Critical Condition," *Tampa Bay Times*, December 2, 1996.

184 *She also underwent an angioplasty procedure*: Ibid.; Telegraph Staff Reporter, "Mother House Turns Mini-Hospital: Sisters Set Up Cardiac Unit as Mother's Heartbeat Remains Erratic," *Telegraph*, September 7, 1996.

185 *Her kidneys, too, were beginning*: AP, "'Cheerful.'"

185 *Calcutta's archbishop, Henry D'Souza, was convinced*: Satinder Bindra, "Archbishop: Mother Teresa Underwent Exorcism," CNN, September 7, 2001, accessed January 4, 2022, https://edition.cnn.com/2001/WORLD/asia pcf/south/09/04/mother.theresa.exorcism/.

185 *At times she would thrash*: Ibid.

185 *Archbishop D'Souza and Father Stroscio had to*: AFP, "Mother Teresa 'Wasn't Possessed by Devils,'" *IOL*, September 9, 2001, accessed January 4, 2022, https://www.iol.co.za/news/world/mother-teresa-wasnt-possessed-by-devils-71918.

185 *"We are not at all sure whether she"*: Sister Nirmala, M.C., Statement to the Press, September 8, 2001.

186 *In 1949, as she was setting out*: Kolodiejchuk, *Mother Teresa*, 134.

186 *The headline the next day was*: Gumbel, "Mother Teresa Pleads."

CHAPTER 14
Going Home

196 *"To live always, without end"*: Benedict XVI, *Spe Salvi* [Encyclical to the Bishops, Priests, and Deacons, Men and Women Religious, and all the Lay Faithful on Christian Hope], November 30, 2007, sec. 10, accessed January 4, 2022, https://www.vatican.va/content/bene dict-xvi/en/encyclicals/documents/hf_ben-xvi_enc _20071130_spe-salvi.html.

196 *Rather than "an unending succession"*: Ibid., sec. 12.

197 *"Abide with me; fast falls the eventide"*: Henry Francis Lyte, "Abide with Me: Fast Falls the Eventide," 1847, Hymnary.org, accessed January 4, 2022, https://hymnary .org/text/abide_with_me_fast_falls_the_eventide.

199 *Four Sisters were particularly focused on caring*: Five Sisters who were present when Mother went home to God—Nirmala, Gertrude, Luke, Nirmala Maria, and Joel, as well as Dr. Alfred Woodward, her longtime personal physician—shared with me their observations of what transpired and together tell the story how she died.

211 *" 'Come, you whom my Father has blessed' "*: Matthew 25:34–40, Jerusalem Bible.

CHAPTER 15
Saint Teresa of Calcutta

213 *At his first public appearance*: Frances D'Emilio, "John Paul II Beseeches God for Just Reward," *Spokesman-Review*, September 7, 1997, accessed January 4, 2022,

https://www.spokesman.com/stories/1997/sep/07/john-paul-ii-beseeches-god-for-just-reward/.

213 *"She lives in my memory as"*: "Pope, World Leaders, Join in Paying Tribute," *Irish Times*, September 8, 1997, accessed January 4, 2022, https://www.irishtimes.com/news/pope-world-leaders-join-in-paying-tribute-1.104075.

213 *Her death, he would say later*: Weigel, *Witness to Hope*, 819.

214 *Just a few weeks after her death*: Ibid.

214 *Within two years, they had assembled*: David Van Biema, "Mother Teresa: The Life and Works of a Modern Saint," *Time*, Updated Reissue of Special Edition, 2016, 81.

216 *I adapted Saint Paul's exhortation*: I Corinthians 11:1.

216 *That pledge sufficed to keep me*: Matthew 26:11.

218 *He knew he would not live*: John Paul II, Homily at the Beatification of Mother Teresa of Calcutta, World Mission Sunday, October 19, 2003, accessed January 4, 2022, https://www.vatican.va/content/john-paul-ii/en/homilies/2003/documents/hf_jp-ii_hom_20031019_mother-theresa.html.

218 *"Let us praise the Lord"*: Ibid.

222 *She saw herself like the "useless"*: Luke 17:7–10.

222 *Her sisters, too, had done*: Matthew 25:34.

224 *At times, I find myself like*: Mark 9:24.

EPILOGUE
The Work Goes On

233 *"Do we know who our own poor are?"*: Kolodiejchuk, *Mother Teresa*, 296.

Index

About the Author

Jim Towey was a trusted adviser and personal friend of Mother Teresa of Calcutta for twelve years, and did the first reading at her Mass of Canonization in Saint Peter's Square. He headed the White House Office of Faith-Based and Community Initiatives under George W. Bush, and was president of two Catholic colleges, a US Senate staffer, and head of Florida's 40,000-employee health and human services agency. In 1996, with Mother Teresa's encouragement, he founded the nonprofit advocacy organization Aging with Dignity and created the Five Wishes advance directive, which has sold 40 million copies and is used in all fifty states. Towey met his wife, Mary, in Mother Teresa's Washington, D.C., AIDS home. He continues to provide pro bono legal services for the Missionaries of Charity.